DON'T
PUT ME IN, COACH

DON'T
PUT ME IN, COACH

MY INCREDIBLE NCAA JOURNEY
from THE END OF THE BENCH
to THE END OF THE BENCH

MARK TITUS

DOUBLEDAY
New York London Toronto
Sydney Auckland

www.doubleday.com

DOUBLEDAY and the portrayal of an anchor with a dolphin
are registered trademarks of Random House, Inc.

Book design by Michael Collica
Jacket design by Michael J. Windsor
Jacket photograph © Deborah Feingold

Insert photographs courtesy of the author

Library of Congress Cataloging-in-Publication Data
Titus, Mark, 1987–
Don't put me in, coach : my incredible NCAA journey from the end of
the bench to the end of the bench / by Mark Titus.
p. cm.
1. Titus, Mark, 1987–
2. Basketball players—United States—Biography.
3. Ohio State Buckeyes (Basketball team)—History.   I. Title.
GV884.T57A3 2011
796.323092—dc23
[B]   2011040854

ISBN 978-0-385-53510-6

MANUFACTURED IN THE UNITED STATES OF AMERICA

3 5 7 9 10 8 6 4

First Edition

For Mom and Dad—
Without your many sacrifices, none of this
would have been possible.

And for the Trillion Man March—
You know I still love you, though we touched
and went our separate ways.

ACKNOWLEDGMENTS

I would be remiss if I didn't thank some people for playing a significant role in my life and helping this book become a reality.

I want to first thank my fiancée for her endless support and for deciding to give a benchwarmer a chance. I want to thank my mom for sacrificing her time and money over the years so I could pursue my dream of playing college basketball, and I want to thank my dad for finding a way to come to every game (home and away) during my senior year at Ohio State, even though he knew I probably wasn't going to play. Special thanks go out to my brother (and his friends) for letting me tag along when I was younger, which is a big reason why I became moderately good at basketball, and much love to my sister for always being my biggest fan. And a shout-out to my best friend since sixth grade, Keller, for being a great sounding board for my ideas and for giving me some good ideas along the way too.

I want to thank all of my teammates, including managers, throughout my life and from every level of every sport I played (especially my Ohio State teammates), for forming friendships and brotherhoods that will last a lifetime. I'll forever be indebted to Coach Matta, all of my assistant coaches at OSU, and The Ohio State University in general for giving me an opportunity that I know I was never entitled to. I want to thank all the Ohio State fans all over the world and the people of Columbus, Ohio, for accepting a Hoosier into the community. I also want to thank my fifth-grade creative writing teacher, Mrs. Boles, for showing me that writing can be fun and doesn't always have to be an arduous process. And a big thank-you goes out to all of the people back in Brownsburg, Indiana, and Danville, Indiana, who supported me even when I was a nobody. There are too many of you to name everyone, but you know who you are.

I want to thank Bill Simmons for giving me my big break, and Jimmy Kimmel for being a mentor for the past couple of years. I also want to thank my agent, James "Babydoll" Dixon, as well as Alex Glass and Scott Trident Media Group, for negotiating a multimillion-dollar book deal for me. And of course, I have to thank all of the fine people at Doubleday, specifically my editors, Jason Kaufman and Robert Bloom, for working hard behind the scenes to make this book much better than it would have been otherwise.

And lastly, I want to thank the Trillion Man March for taking me on an unbelievable ride that I'll never forget as long as I live. You guys are awesome. But you knew that already.

DON'T

PUT ME IN, COACH

PROLOGUE

I woke up on the morning of August 28, 2009, in Windsor, Ontario, with groggy eyes and a pesky morning wood I couldn't seem to get rid of.

Undaunted, I crawled out of bed and slowly made my way down the hallway to the bathroom. I positioned myself in front of the toilet, lowered my underpants, and emptied a stream of urine into the bowl, although nearly half of it ended up on the seat. *Sucks for whoever has to clean that up*, I thought before flushing the toilet and returning to my room, where I crawled back into bed and played a game on my cell phone for at least a half-hour.

Yes, August 28, 2009, started like most days typically do for me. Little did I know, though, that by the time I got back into that same bed later that night, it would certainly end up being anything but a typical day.

I was about to start my senior and final season as a walk-on benchwarmer for the Ohio State basketball team, and I was in Windsor because our team had traveled there a couple of days earlier to play the University of Windsor and the University of Western Ontario in a few exhibition games. Even though it was still the off-season and most American college basketball teams weren't allowed to practice together yet, we were able to play in Windsor because of an NCAA rule that allows teams to make international trips during the off-season once every few years to play foreign competition. And yes, teams are permitted to go just about anywhere in the world on these trips, yet we chose to go to a place that was five minutes away from America and, at just a four-hour drive, was literally the closest foreign soil to our campus in Columbus, Ohio. In other words, this was an "international trip" in the same way that OJ was "not guilty"—I wasn't buying it, even though pretty much all of the black guys were.

The first game on our trip was to be later that night against the University of Windsor, who we were actually scheduled to play the following night as well. Throughout the day leading up to this first game, I was certain of two things. First of all, I knew for an absolute fact that we would destroy Windsor because, well, they were Canadians, and if there are two things that I can think of that Canadians are historically not very good at, they are basketball and beating Americans. (I tease you because I love you, Canada.) And secondly, because I knew that we would easily beat Windsor, I was also absolutely certain that I would get to play in the game. As a walk-on benchwarmer for the team, I typically only saw the court during games when there were only a few minutes left and our team was in the midst of a blowout. It seemed to me that this game would qualify as one of those times, so I spent all day mentally and physically getting prepared.

Now, to an outsider, playing for just a handful of minutes in a game in which the outcome has already been decided might not seem like much, but for most of us walk-ons it can be a pretty nerve-wracking experience. After all, when it's time for us to check into the game we've typically been sitting on the bench for a couple of hours and are therefore in no way warmed up or physically prepared to play high-level basketball. Plus, since we're walk-ons, it can be assumed that even if we were properly stretched and warmed up, we'd still be much less athletic and much less talented than all the other guys on the court, so really, we're at a huge disadvantage from the start.

But most importantly, what makes the experience so nerve-wracking is the fact that there are thousands of people in the stands and it seems like just about every one of them wants to see us make at least one shot, most likely because nothing conveys complete dominance over another team quite like walk-ons scoring. In reality, what we do on the court is completely trivial because nobody really remembers or cares all that much the next day whether or not the walk-ons scored, but it doesn't matter to us. No matter how many times we do it, each and every game that we play in feels like it's the Super Bowl and every single person in the building has their eyes locked in on us. And even though it's probably entirely unwarranted, there truly is an enormous pressure that comes with this.

On this particular day, it seemed like that pressure was getting to me a little bit. That, or it was the trip the day before to the Canadian McDonald's, where I got a little carried away with my amazement at the concept of a Double Big Mac and ended up eating two of them. Either way, on the day of our first game I found myself fighting a serious battle with my bowels, and judging from the fact that I had spent most of the day on the toilet, I'd say my bowels were winning. I already had some butterflies in my stomach from knowing that I was about to play in my first international basketball game and—because of an injury I suffered the season before—my first basketball game of any kind in over a year. But now I was facing a serious crisis because the butterflies in my stomach had some company in the form of explosive diarrhea.

My stomach got so bad that when the game finally rolled around, I had to excuse myself from my spot on the bench during the first half so I could return to the locker room bathroom and take care of some business. By that time I had spent the better part of the day on the toilet and my bunghole was consequently a little tender, but I really had no choice but to suck it up because the fact of the matter was that I was going to have to find a way to get ready to play the last few minutes of the game. There was simply no way around it. No matter how much I might have not wanted to go into the game, the bottom line was that I was a walk-on who rarely got any playing time, so I had no choice but to take the opportunity to play whenever I could get it. Plus, it wasn't like I could turn down my head coach, Thad Matta, when he asked me to check in. That's because it was understood that a walk-on doing such a thing would require a huge set of brass balls, since it would give the head coach the impression that we really didn't care about getting better at basketball and weren't taking our role on the team seriously. In short, despite my digestive problems, I was going to have to play high-level college basketball in front of a few thousand people in less than an hour and there was nothing I could do to prevent it.

As the game reached its final stages, the tension was so thick it seemed tangible, not so much because the outcome of the game hung in the balance—we had at least a 50-point lead—but more because I knew Coach Matta was inevitably going to tell me to check in at any moment. Then, with about three minutes left on the clock and our lead holding steady at around 50 points, it happened. He stood up from his spot at the head of the bench and walked down to the end of the bench I was occupying. "You ready to go in?" he asked. I momentarily froze.

I took a deep breath, looked up at him, and said:

"Nah, I'm good."

As soon as the words left my mouth, I couldn't believe I had the gall to actually go through with it. This wasn't the first time I would have rather just sat on the bench as the game's final minutes ticked away instead of actually playing a little bit. But even when I didn't feel like playing, I always responded with an enthusiastic "Yep!" and peeled off my warm-ups as I darted off the bench. I don't know whether the diarrhea had screwed with my brain or the fact that I was a senior made me feel a false sense of power, but something came over me and told me that now was the time to pull out my brass balls for all the world to see. Now was the time to finally tell Coach Matta I wanted to stay on the bench. There was no turning back now.

Naturally, Coach Matta was taken aback by my response. He replied, "You're good? You don't want to play?"

Unsure of whether or not he was pissed, I added a little more detail. "Yeah, I'm good right here. I had stomach trouble all day, and my butthole is on fire right now because of it. I just really don't feel like running around out there with a fiery butthole, you know?"

"You're serious, aren't you?"

"I'm dead serious, Coach. We're playing the same team tomorrow night, so why don't we just wait until then for me to play?"

He shook his head, let out a laugh, and returned to the other end of the bench. The next night I played three minutes and scored three points in our rematch against Windsor, and the incident was never spoken of again.

And just like that, I made walk-on history. Not only did I tell my head coach I wasn't going to go into the game because I didn't feel like it, but I also didn't get reprimanded in the slightest. I had already established myself as a bit of a pioneer in the walk-on community because of the blog I had started writing a year earlier, but in that moment I instantly became a walk-on revolutionary. I had just disregarded the unwritten rules for walk-ons and done something so inconceivably foolish that no one had ever even attempted it before me. But I didn't just attempt the impossible—I conquered it, and in the process set a new precedent for all walk-ons who were to follow me.

Yes, August 28, 2009, certainly ended up being anything but a typical day. But that's probably because I was anything but a typical college basketball walk-on.

My name is Mark Titus, and this is my story.

PART ONE

People who have the least to do with the success of
a team often have the most to say about it.

—*Larry Bird*
When the Game Was Ours (2009)

ONE

nybody who has ever been a walk-on for a Division I football or basketball team will tell you that being likened to Rudy at least once during a four-year career is pretty much an inevitability. The general public hears the term "walk-on" and immediately thinks that anyone who couldn't earn a scholarship must have been told his entire life that he wasn't good enough, before he relentlessly annoyed coaches for a spot on the team and got life-changing advice from what has to be the wisest field maintenance guy to ever live.

Sadly, this image of a short, white walk-on caring more about the success of the team than all of his teammates combined is reinforced every March, when the guys wearing all their warm-ups on the end of the bench react to routine plays in the NCAA Tournament like tween girls at a Bieber concert. These douchers ruin it for the rest of us, as they cement a stereotype for all walk-ons that forever perpetuates the Rudy comparison. Well, you're never going to believe this, but not all walk-ons actually fit this description. I know, I know. It's hard to wrap your mind around the fact that there are sometimes exceptions to stereotypes, but you're just going to have to trust me with this one.

I was fully aware of the walk-on stereotype when I started my career at Ohio State, which is why I promised myself that I would do everything in my power to be an exception. Don't get me wrong, I think *Rudy* is full of all sorts of inspiration and is the second-best sports movie ever made. (I'm from Indiana and played basketball—I'll let you guess what I think the best sports movie of all time is.) But I've found that very few people make a Rudy comparison in a complimentary way. Instead, they seem to be saying, "I think it's adorable how you try really hard even though you suck balls and there's no way you'll ever get a chance to play." This is why, from day one, I tried to distance myself from the Rudy comparison by pulling pranks on superstar teammates, routinely falling asleep during film sessions, and basically spending every day with the team trying to figure out exactly how much I could get away with. And as it turned out, I could get away with a lot.

Whenever I reminisce with my friends and family about my four years of being a dickhead at Ohio State, they always seem to ask how exactly I was capable of getting away with some of the things I did. (Don't worry, we'll cover all of my shenanigans later.) After all, I was the bottom-feeder on the team who was supposed to just keep his mouth shut and stand on the sideline during practice until a coach told me to step in for a drill and essentially get sodomized in my role as human punching bag. You'd think that it would only take one screwup on my part for Coach Matta to send my ass packing, but instead he seemed to embrace me as the comedic relief for the team.

In the history of the walk-on–head coach relationship, this was unprecedented. Never had someone in my position been given the freedom I was given, which is why I felt a great responsibility to use this privilege to my advantage. Which brings us back to the original question: how did I go from being a math major basketball manager who knew only three people on campus to one of the loudest voices in the locker room of the number-one-ranked college basketball team in less than a month? The answer to that lies deeply buried in a story about drugs, prostitution, love, betrayal, organized crime in the 1920s, and one man's pursuit of the American Dream.

And by that I mean that the answer has nothing to do with any of those things. Sorry if I got your hopes up.

TWO

I don't want to brag or anything, but I honestly can't remember getting my first pubes. You might be confused as to how this could possibly be bragging, which is why I should also mention that I vividly remember third grade. Now, I don't want to jump to conclusions, but it seems like since I can remember third grade but I can't remember getting pubes, I must have started puberty before third grade. In other words, I had at least a two-year head start on the rest of my classmates in the race to become the guy all the ladies wanted to tongue-kiss under the bleachers at the varsity football games.

I towered over all my friends, and I was even taller than most of my brother's friends, despite them being three years older than me. In fact, I was so much bigger than other kids my age that I had to get a special desk made for me in elementary school because I couldn't fit in the regular desks. Seriously. I was basically just like Robin Williams in *Jack*, only I wasn't completely covered with hair, and instead of being socially awkward about my size I dunked on fools on the seven-foot rims during recess. (Also, I wouldn't have completely blown the chance to get it on with Fran Drescher like Jack did, but that's a discussion we'll have to save for another time.)

My size made me a natural fit for basketball, and I quickly fell in love with the game. Since my dad was the athletic director at a local high school when I was growing up, I always had access to a gym and would often stay for hours after the high school games on Friday and Saturday nights to shoot around. Sure this mostly consisted of me throwing up half-court shots and trying to drop-kick the ball in from the top row of the stands, but that's not the point. The point is that I sacrificed my Friday nights and therefore never got the chance to get a pants tent from watching Topanga during *TGIF*, all because I wanted to get in the gym, work on my game, and try to get better so I could make it to the NBA someday. Besides, those half-courters and shots from the bleachers proved to be useful years later when I made "Mr. Rainmaker," my critically acclaimed YouTube video.

All this "practice" also paid off in the short term, as I instantly became a beast in the local rec league. But after a few years of playing in a league with just kids from my town, I ended up quitting because (a) the refs were dads of other kids in the league, which is to say they secretly despised me for destroying their sons and took out their frustration by calling criminally unfair fouls on me, and (b) our league had a limit on the number of points one person could score in a game. That's right—the league punished kids for being talented, which is the most ass-backwards philosophy I've ever heard of. What kind of Communist thought process was behind this decision to deter success in the interest of fairness? Last time I checked, this is America. And in America it's not only encouraged to beat up on the little guys to get ahead in life—it's necessary. Anyway, just so we're clear, I'm blaming my lack of an NBA career on the cheesedicks in charge of my youth rec league. They put handcuffs on me at an early age, and I never was able to break free from them.

I reached my boiling point with the rec league when I blocked the shot of some dweeb who wore shirts with wizards and dragons on them and the refs called me for yet another bogus foul, only because I was a foot taller than the other kid. Instead of throwing a tantrum and causing a scene like most kids my age would have done, I waited until the game started again, sat down at half-court, took my shoes off, and cried for my mom in the bleachers to take me home. (Remember, kids: always take the high road.) Sure my outburst was ridiculous, but there was solid reasoning behind my behavior, considering it was obvious to me that the rec league wasn't challenging me enough and I was in desperate need of better competition. Ya know, competition that didn't play in jean shorts or keep an inhaler in its back pocket during the game. Thanks to AAU basketball, I more than found what I was looking for.

For those who don't know, the Amateur Athletic Union oversees tournaments all over the country for amateur athletes in a variety of sports. But in basketball circles, "AAU" is basically just another way of saying "club basketball," as the fundamental idea behind AAU teams is that they are made up of the best players from several towns and even states, as opposed to teammates coming from just one town. The truth is that AAU governs only a very small fraction of the hundreds of tournaments that players could potentially play in during any given summer, but since it is the foremost organization in amateur sports, its name is synonymous with summer basketball. When I started playing AAU in 1997, it wasn't nearly as huge as it is now—some kids today would rather play AAU during the summer than play for their school teams—but it was still a good opportunity for me to test my skills against the best. More importantly, it gave me a chance to not feel like an ogre for being the only one on the court with armpit hair.

to practice shooting threes and weren't all that great at it. Knowing this, we basically forced them to match our style of play, and for a while the game turned into a three-point contest that featured them bricking shot after shot and us having the exact amount of success that you would think white guys from Indiana would have. Eventually, they figured our zone out and turned up their defensive intensity when the game mattered most, but for a quick second we gave them a scare that would have surely turned the seventh-grade AAU basketball world upside down. Even though we ran out of gas down the stretch and came up a little short, we managed to expose a serious flaw in a seemingly flawless team and only lost by seven, which was by far the closest any team had come to beating them up to that point.

So, how did this game "change my life forever," or whatever dramatic phrase I used earlier to make this story sound more interesting? Well, what I failed to previously mention is that I was a mismatch nightmare for Greg and Mike's team and played out of my mind for most of the game. As a six-foot-two seventh-grader with a wet jumper, I was too big for little guys like Mike to guard me, and I was too good of a shooter for big guys like Greg, who usually never leave the paint on defense, to guard me. I was essentially a junior-high version of Dirk Nowitzki, all the way down to the fact that I also considered Detlef Schrempf a personal hero of mine (but only because his flat top was damn near immaculate—not quite on the same level as Chris Mullin's, but then again, whose is?). I lit Mike and Greg's team up to the tune of 18 points and 7 rebounds (and no assists because passing is entirely unnecessary), which doesn't sound like much at first, but when you consider that high school band parties have twice as much scoring as a typical seventh-grade basketball game, it arguably becomes just as impressive as Wilt's 100 or Kobe's 81.

My performance was so impressive, in fact, that Mike's dad, who was Mike and Greg's coach, asked me to join their team at the end of the AAU season, after our game made him realize that the lack of a good outside shooter could lead to their demise. Since I was deadly from downtown and was projected to be six-nine by the time I was a senior in high school, Mike Sr. figured I was the missing piece to their puzzle of basketball perfection. Unfortunately for him, he figured wrong. I essentially stopped growing, my athleticism somehow deteriorated, and I became such a one-dimensional player that even Antoine Walker would have thought I shot too many threes.

But that wasn't until later on down the road. For the time being, what was important was that I had my foot in the door and was now a member of the best AAU team in the country. The opportunities that came with this would prove to be staggering, as there's no way in hell I ever would have played at Ohio State, become one of the most famous walk-ons of all time (which, let's be honest, is like being the smartest Kardashian), or been given a book deal to talk about it all had I never been on that AAU team. Basically, my entire identity would have been completely different from what it is today. So yeah, that's how one game changed my life forever.

FOUR

s I walked into the gym for my first practice with my new AAU team, I decided it was crucial to send a message to my teammates that I wasn't there to dick around. I accomplished this by pulling a pistol out of my bag, firing three shots in the air, and declaring to everyone in the most badass way imaginable that "you assholes picked a good day to die." And by that I mean that I kept to myself and didn't really talk to anyone because I was so terrified.

Being the only white guy in the gym (they added another white guy to the team, but he lived an hour from Indy and never came to any of our practices) was a huge culture shock for me, considering that my school had a total of one nonwhite student, but only after adding together the two biracial kids. It wasn't so much that I was a racist little kid, but rather that getting dropped into this new culture felt like a whirlwind and I wasn't exactly mature enough to adapt to the change. These guys played a different style of basketball, talked differently, dressed differently, and had different off-the-court interests than I did. I was completely overwhelmed and thought for sure I'd never be able to fit in with any of my new teammates. And then Greg introduced himself.

If it weren't for Wayne Brady, John Howard Griffin, and Carlton Banks, the young version of Greg Oden could very well make a case for being the whitest black person to ever live. Clearly I don't mean that he had light pigmentation for a black guy, but rather that he seemed to identify more with white culture than he did with black culture. Whereas most black basketball players aim to be the epitome of cool, Greg used to play in Rec-Specs and routinely wore calf-high socks with jean shorts. I would say that he was kind of a goober, but I've never actually used the word "goober" in my life, and I don't want to start now, so I'll instead just say he looked like a dweeb. As we got older, Greg stayed true to his adopted culture by watching *Laguna Beach* religiously (I know this because we discussed Team Kristin versus Team LC far more often than two straight men ever should), and he even came to my high school's prom instead of his own because there were "too many black people" at his school's prom.

But my favorite example of Greg shying away from his natural culture came in the summer before our senior year of high school. We had an off day during the week of a tournament in Las Vegas, and most of the guys on the team tried to convince their parents to take them to an Ashanti concert. Hell, even I wanted to go until I found out that Ja Rule wasn't going to be there too. (Sorry, Ashanti, but as far as I'm concerned you can either sing "Mesmerize" with Ja Rule or you can STFU.) But when my dad suggested that we go see a matinee magic show on the Strip instead, my inner nerd came out and decided that that was a much better idea. When I mentioned to Greg what my dad and I planned on doing, he immediately asked if he could come with us.

That's right—when given the choice between a concert featuring one of the best R&B singers at the time and a $15 matinee magic show, Greg picked the magic show without hesitation. This single decision contradicted every stereotype I ever had about black basketball players and helped subdue all of the uneasiness I had about integrating with my new teammates.

Because Greg and I shared a lot of similar interests other than basketball, I tended to hang out with him off the court more than I did with any of my other teammates. Some have suggested that the two of us really didn't have that much in common and I was just forging a friendship because I knew he was going to be a millionaire NBA player in a few years, which is an accusation I can't fully deny. But I swear that wasn't the only reason. (You gotta believe me!) The way I see it, if Greg was Vince Chase, I was much more like E than I was like Turtle, if for no other reason than I like to think that I actually brought something to the table, even if I could never figure out exactly what that something was.

Either way, my friendship with Greg played a pivotal role in my attempt to integrate with my teammates, especially since I was having just as tough of a time trying to fit in on the court as I was off of it. That's because, even though I was successfully fulfilling my role as designated three-point specialist, my playing time fluctuated more than a sine wave with an angular frequency of $1,000\pi$ radians per second. (That's a nerd joke from a former math major, bitch.) Some games I would play just about every minute and even occasionally lead the team in scoring, and then others I wouldn't even get off the bench. I understood that my playing time almost exclusively depended on the style of play of our opponent, which is to say it almost exclusively depended on how many white guys were on the other team, but that didn't make it any less frustrating. My unpredictable playing time did, however, make things occasionally entertaining.

If there's one story I love telling more than any other about my time on the best AAU team ever assembled, it has to be how I used to room on the road with Daequan Cook (who played with me for a year at Ohio State and now plays for the Oklahoma City Thunder), and he would stay up until four in the morning shooting dice with Aaron Pogue (who played at Cleveland State) while *Friday* blared on the TV in the background and I desperately tried to get sleep to prepare for our 8:00 a.m. game. But if there are two stories I love to tell, they are that one and what I'm going to tell you with these next few paragraphs.

Less than a month after I had torched the second-best AAU team in Indiana for 27 points in a tournament in Indianapolis, I found myself glued to the bench during the championship game of the prestigious Houston Kingwood Classic Tournament. Because Josh McRoberts (who now plays for the Los Angeles Lakers) had been added to our team earlier that year and was a senior while the rest of us were either juniors or sophomores, we were forced to play teams that were older than almost all of our players. Nonetheless, we breezed through the tournament with relative ease before meeting up with Lou Williams (who now plays for the Philadelphia 76ers) and the Georgia Stars in the championship. The Stars had zero white guys on their team, which meant there was nobody for me to guard, so I had an idea before the game that I most likely wouldn't even need to bother warming up. I was spot-on with my prediction.

For 39 minutes and 45 seconds, the game was a back-and-forth battle in which I didn't even sniff the court. Then, with 15 seconds left and us down by three with the ball, Mike's dad called time-out and told me to check in. Naturally, I was caught off guard by this, but I wasn't all that worried because I figured I wouldn't have to do much more than stand in the corner while the good players made something happen. Instead, as I made my way back to the huddle from the scorer's table, Mike Sr. looked me square in the eye and said, "Get ready. We need you to hit this," before drawing up a play that would lead to me sinking a three to send it to overtime. Most guys in my situation (hadn't played the entire game, ice-cold legs, championship on the line) would have been so nervous they would have soiled their trousers. But not me. As we broke from the huddle, I had a focused look on my face as I grabbed a fistful of Mike Sr.'s shirt and firmly said, "Coach, I got this."

Lou Williams noticed that I had probably checked into the

game solely because I was a good shooter and we were going to run a play for me, and therefore decided that since he was their best player, he should be the one to guard me. As soon as I stepped on the court, he attached himself to my hip, as if to say there was no way in hell I was going to even get the game-tying shot off, let alone make it. But despite his best efforts, he was no match for me on this particular play. As the clock ticked down to less than 10 seconds, I came off a double screen, left him in the dust, and ran to the corner to spot up. While this was happening, Mike swung the ball to Daequan at the top of the key, just like we drew it up in the time-out. Once I got my feet set and my shoulders squared to the basket, I locked eyes with Daequan and raised my eyebrows to let him know I was ready for the pass.

During that moment, time seemed to slow down as my thoughts raced through my mind. *Am I really about to make the biggest shot of the game after sitting on the bench for all but 15 seconds? Why did Coach draw a play up for me even though we have five future NBA players on our team? And if the other team knew the play was for me, how did I get so open?* I was entirely aware that this was the most important shot in my life and it was literally one second away from happening. It all came down to this.

With just a few seconds left on the clock, Daequan saw that I was open and took two dribbles toward me to make the pass easier for him. He then picked up his dribble, faked a pass in my direction, shot a fadeaway with two guys in his face, and stared in amazement as his shot barely grazed the rim and the buzzer echoed throughout the gym.

Game over. We lose. Just like we drew it up.

Even though he squashed my potential moment of glory, I eventually forgave Daequan for not passing to me. Chances are that I would have missed the shot anyway, so it actually worked out well that I can now just place all the blame on him instead of having to search for an excuse for my failure, and that's really all that matters. Besides, there were way too many good memories from my years of playing AAU to care all that much about this one minor setback. It was without a doubt the most fun I've ever had playing basketball, and rightfully so considering we had the best AAU team of all time, which isn't so much my opinion as it is a fact. (Our starting five of Mike Conley, Eric Gordon, Daequan Cook, Josh McRoberts, and Greg Oden are all in the NBA and are all either playing huge roles for their teams or have had full-body pictures of themselves wearing nothing but a do-rag leaked on the internet.)

When I finally got to know my teammates better, I discovered that we actually had a lot in common, and I became good friends with most of them. Even to this day I keep in touch with a lot of guys from that team, although that might change with a couple of them after they read this book. Either way, I'll always cherish my time with that team because it was the first time in my life that I felt a sense of brotherhood with people other than my actual brother. This kinship was so important to me, in fact, that when three of my teammates committed to Ohio State, I decided to apply there as a safety school in case my own basketball recruitment didn't work out, even though I knew nothing about the school and had never even seen the campus. As it turned out, this was a great decision on my part because I was in desperate need of a safety school when my recruitment to Harvard wasn't the done deal I thought it was and ended up going down in flames rather quickly.

FIVE

Other than having an immaculate stubble-beard and being hung like a stallion, the one characteristic of mine that I'm most proud of is my refusal to take things too seriously. I'm a strict believer in the philosophy that life is way too short to do anything but have as much fun as you possibly can. Sure it's a philosophy that makes me just as mature and responsible as the cast of *Jersey Shore*, but it's also a philosophy that makes me an enjoyable person to be around. Simply put, I'm only on this earth for a short period of time, and I'd rather spend that time being happy than stressing out over dumb things like "having a job" or "paying child support."

Now, like any red-blooded American, I do have some pet peeves that piss me off to no end (such as writers who put parentheses in the middle of sentences and consequently ruin the flow of the sentence, discovering a lack of toilet paper while on the toilet, and terrorism, just to name a few), but that doesn't change the fact that my main focus in life is to have a blast and not let things bother me too much. When I was at Ohio State, I was welcomed with open arms by Coach Matta because I helped keep the team loose. Since I never played, I wasn't expected to take things as seriously as the scholarship players and was therefore allowed a little freedom to screw around, which ended up being great for (mostly) everyone. In high school, though, it was a completely different story. My same attitude toward life that was celebrated at Ohio State was frowned upon at Brownsburg High because, believe it or not, I was the best player on our team.

Looking back, my biggest problem throughout my basketball career was always that I never thought of basketball as anything other than a game, primarily because it isn't anything other than a game. While I do have a competitive side to me, my motivation for being good at basketball never was that I wanted to be the best. I was motivated to get better solely because being good made the game more enjoyable, kinda like how most guys who play video games don't necessarily want to be the best at "Halo" or "Madden," but rather just want to be good enough to make it consistently fun. So when my high school hired a new coach before my junior year who was a young guy trying to establish himself as a bit of a hard-ass, well, I guess you could say we butted heads.

As the head coach at a big high school in the most basketball-crazed state in America, his focus was on making everyone on our team the best basketball players we possibly could be, which is why he held preseason workouts at 6:00 a.m. before school started. And as a 17-year-old high school junior who only cared about stealing gas money from my mom's purse and looking at boobs on the internet (some things never change), my focus was on doing everything in my power to not have to go to these workouts. The reality is that I'm not sure I'd wake up at 5:30 in the morning even if I somehow knew that my family had been taken hostage, so it goes without saying that I wanted no part of waking up that early to play basketball. Luckily for me, I was the quarterback of the football team and could always use football as an excuse for not being able to go to basketball workouts. (I'm not saying this was the only reason I played football, but I'm also not saying it wasn't.) Even though I technically could have gone to basketball in the morning and football after school, I thought that doing so would contradict my philosophy of not taking things too seriously and thus decided that the 6:00 a.m. workouts could suck it. My coach wasn't exactly thrilled with this decision.

When basketball season finally arrived, our conflicting mentalities became even more of an issue. All of us who thought we had signed up to play basketball suddenly found ourselves constantly running sprints, doing defensive slides, or lifting weights. I'd been wrong before, but it seemed to me that it would have been a good idea to use an actual basketball if he was trying to help us become better basketball players. My teammates felt the same way about these practices. Our collective feeling could best be summed up with Kenny Powers's quote to Principal Cutler: "I play real sports. I'm not trying to be the best at exercising."

I mean, it's not like I wanted to play grab-ass every day at practice. It's just that when the varsity guys consistently got yelled at for little things like making fun of the JV guys, I realized that a serious problem existed. (What's the point of even playing high school sports if you can't haze the younger guys?) As the leader of the team (and as a guy who has a bad habit of being brutally honest), I felt a responsibility to voice the team's collective frustration to our coach. I accomplished this in a one-on-one meeting I had with him, during which he asked me how the guys on the team felt about him and I told him point-blank, "We all think you're an asshole and you're taking all the fun away from basketball," which, coincidentally, is the exact same thing I told Evan Turner just about every day at Ohio State. Surprisingly, my coach didn't look that upset, but I could still tell that I had done some pretty irreversible damage. After all, it's common knowledge that calling your coach an asshole to his face is at least a seven on a scale from one to Spreewell.

Even though Coach wasn't visibly upset at the time, in the next few weeks he set the tone for the rest of my high school career by taking out all of his frustrations with the team on me. When guys were late for 8:00 a.m. Saturday practices, it was my fault because

I was the team leader and I should have been the one to call them in the morning to wake them up. When our team lacked defensive intensity in practice and started to get schooled by the JV team, I was the one who was supposed to get everyone to pull their heads out of their asses. Hell, I even expected to get yelled at when one of my teammates got caught littering and smoking the reefer. Virtually everyone on the team hated his tough-guy approach (three guys quit within the first month of practice), but I took all the heat because I had the balls to tell him to lighten the F up. What's worse, when he confronted the entire team and told anyone who had a problem with him to speak up, my teammates hung me out to dry by keeping their heads down and their mouths shut. (I hope you're reading this, guys—you're all a bunch of pussies.)

Because of this, our coach unfairly labeled me as lazy, since he was under the impression that I was the only one who thought his practices were too strenuous. The way he saw it, I had a terrible work ethic and wanted to play kickball every day in practice while all of my teammates busted their balls to make our team better. My response was twofold. First of all, who in their right mind wouldn't rather play kickball than run sprints? It's f'ing kickball. If the worst part about growing up is getting all sorts of unwanted body hair, the second-worst part about growing up has to be that kickball isn't as socially acceptable as it is when you're younger. In high school, kickball is second only to dodgeball as everyone's favorite game in gym class, but if you ask guys in college to play kickball, they'll almost certainly respond with "Nah, that's gay. Let's go get drunk instead." So excuse me for wanting to play kickball while I still could.

Secondly, I wasn't lazy so much as I was normal. I worked on my game more than anyone on the team, but since I, like every other person on our team, wasn't a fan of conditioning for 30 minutes every day after practice (or playing any defense whatsoever), I couldn't shake the "lazy" tag from my coach's mind. Throughout the next year and a half, we frequently butted heads over my perceived lack of work ethic, but nothing serious ever came of it. That is, until the tail end of my senior year.

Toward the end of my high school basketball career, it became clear to me that the only chance I had at playing college basketball was if I went to Harvard. I was recruited by all sorts of mid-major schools from all over the country, but I told them pretty much from the start that I wasn't interested because I had grown up in a Big Ten family and had always wanted to go to a school from one of the six BCS conferences. That wasn't to say that I thought I was above playing mid-major basketball, but was more of a reflection on my view of the college experience as a whole, as I grew up always wanting to go to a school with a huge student population and a huge campus whether I played basketball or not. The obvious problem with this, though, was that I simply wasn't good enough to get basketball scholarship offers from big schools, so I was left stuck in the middle ground of not good enough and not interested.

But after I gave it some thought I realized that I really did want to play basketball in college, so I gave Harvard a chance only because it was Harvard and I was apparently a pretentious dick when I was in high school. Harvard's coaches started recruiting me during the spring of my junior year, shortly after I averaged 17 points per game on the court and off the court scored a 2000 on my SAT (missed one f'ing question on the math section both times I took it). After they watched me make it rain a handful of times with my AAU team during the summer, it seemed pretty obvious that my combination of skills and smarts (for a basketball player anyway) made them all moist in their panties. They called me about once a week for the rest of the summer and eventually had me on campus for a visit. After my visit I was pretty set on going to Harvard, but their coaches wanted to watch me play in one last high school game before making their decision about me.

In the week leading up to the game, my coach and I got into yet another argument. This time he was upset because he thought I wasn't rebounding as well as I should've been, even though I was a small forward/shooting guard who was averaging 5.5 rebounds per game (or 4.5 more rebounds than should have been expected of me). Everything boiled over when I failed to follow my shot during a scrimmage and he stopped practice to ream into me like never before. I calmly explained that the reason I never followed my shot was because I expected the ball to go through the basket every time I shot it. (This was always my pet peeve with coaches—no good shooter in the history of the game ever consistently ran toward the basket as soon as he shot the ball.) He didn't take too kindly to me talking back and decided to take the argument to another level by bringing up other problems he had with me. At this point, my blood really started to boil and I may or may not have told him to go fist himself.

Back and forth we traded verbal blows for another few rounds, and when the dust finally settled I had been kicked out of practice and suspended for the entire first half of the game the Harvard coaches were coming to. (It should be noted that he had known for over two weeks that the Harvard coaches were coming to that game.) I begged and pleaded for him to make me run thousands of sprints instead, but it was to no avail. When the game rolled around, I served my time as I sat on the bench the entire first half and noticed that the Harvard coaches in the stands were visibly frustrated. Then, when I came out of the locker room and returned to the court after halftime, they were gone and I never heard from them again. I ended up scoring 13 points in the second half, and we squeaked out a close game, but it was all for naught. My only opportunity at playing college basketball was up in smoke.

Throughout my career at Ohio State, I was often introduced to people as "the guy who turned down Harvard for the chance to be a Buckeye." I obviously never corrected anyone who said this, because being known as the guy who turned down Harvard was like being known as a guy who turned down an orgy at the Playboy mansion. People respected me much more than they would have otherwise, since they thought I must really have a lot going for me if I told the most prestigious college in America that they weren't good enough. Well, now you all know the truth. In no way did I turn down Harvard. But just so we're clear, if everyone wants to continue believing that I did, I'll be perfectly fine with that.

I had originally applied to Ohio State only because Greg, Mike, and Daequan committed there, but the more I looked into the school the more I realized it was a perfect fit. Upon learning that I was going to join him at OSU, Greg used his power as the number-one recruit in the country to persuade the coaches to not only let us be roommates in our dorm but to also let me be a manager on the basketball team. In the end, we never actually roomed together because as soon as the coaches offered Greg a dorm that would come with his own bedroom instead of the shared bedroom that our dorm room would have had, he kicked me to the curb. (After hearing all about his sex life every day at practice, this turned out to be a huge blessing in disguise.) Nonetheless, I did become a manager for the basketball team, which was something I agreed to do only because one of the assistant coaches told me that being a manager meant I would be on the practice squad and get to play against the real team every day in practice. It didn't take long for me to realize that this was a bold-faced lie.

SIX

I first met Coach Matta 20 minutes before my first practice as team manager my freshman year. He came into the gym a half-hour early to walk around and greet the handfuls of people who were there to watch practice, which was kind of surprising to me. Since I knew next to nothing about him, I watched him closely so that I'd have some sort of idea of what to say to him.

I instantly noticed that every person he talked to seemed like the funniest person to ever live, because at some point during every conversation Coach Matta would burst into hysterical laughter. Seeing this again and again made me nervous that I was supposed to have a joke lined up for when I ultimately met him. I rummaged through my brain for the perfect joke to make him laugh harder than the others that people were throwing at him, but everything I thought of was either racist, extremely offensive, or racist.

Left without an appropriate joke, a sense of defeat came over me as Coach Matta introduced himself.

"Hey, Mark, good to meet you. Let me ask you something. Do you know how I got into coaching?" I obviously didn't know, and

I was completely thrown off guard that he would ask me that, but before I could think of a response, he started with his answer:

"Well, my first job out of college was a greeter at Wal-Mart. I think I might have been the only greeter in the history of the company who was younger than 95, but whatever. I made what I thought was decent money, and it was easy work. Until one day this fat, ugly bitch of a woman came into the store with her two kids. She was cussing at them, and I even saw her smack one of the kids in the face as they were walking in. Just the worst mother and one of the worst people I've ever seen in my life. So when she came in, I decided I'd put her in her place. I said hello, told her that her kids were adorable, and asked her if they were twins. She looked at me like I was crazy and said, 'Are you blind or just retarded? Of course they aren't twins. One is ten and the other is six. What the hell would make you think that they were twins?' I said, 'I'm sorry, ma'am, but I just couldn't figure out why in the world someone would want to screw you twice.' "

As soon as he hit his punch line, Coach Matta busted into laughter and walked away, leaving me speechless.

Everything suddenly made sense—he hadn't been laughing with everyone he talked to because he was laughing at *their* jokes. No, he was laughing at *his own* joke. I was stunned and immediately knew that he and I would have no problems getting along. In less than a minute after meeting the guy, he had already told me a joke that hit my trifecta of joke-telling: pass the joke off as if it's a true story, make sure the joke is so corny/dumb that the average person will groan, and finish it off by laughing louder than your entire audience combined. Not only did he execute all three flawlessly, but he took the joke to a whole new level by failing to reach a logical conclusion, since he started by asking me if I knew how he got into coaching and then proceeded to tell a story that in no way explained how he got into coaching. It was pure genius and damn near brought a tear to my eye.

Once I found out that Coach Matta and I had the exact same sense of humor, my nervousness subsided and I became genuinely excited about my role as team manager. All it took for this to change, though, was quickly discovering that "being on the practice team" was apparently another way for OSU basketball coaches to say "doing nothing but bitch work." Sure I was naive to think I would actually practice with the team every day, but that doesn't change the fact that I was entirely lied to and ended up doing everything I wanted to avoid. Instead of making it rain in practice, my responsibilities included filling up and handing out water bottles, wiping up sweat off the floor, rebounding for any player who asked me to, and doing anything else that needed to be done but nobody actually wanted to do.

After about a week and a half, I made up some excuse about how I wanted to concentrate on my studies (more like concentrate on all those college babes, am I right?) when I told the graduate assistant who was in charge of all the managers that I was quitting and he could S my D. Don't get me wrong; it's not like I thought I was too good to be a manager or anything like that. I think college basketball managers are doing the Lord's work and don't get anywhere near the credit they deserve. Shoot, some of my favorite people from my four years at Ohio State were basketball managers (no—not you, Barrale), so I have a ton of respect for them and would have had no problem doing what they do. It's just that . . . ah hell, who am I kidding? Of course I thought I was too good to be a manager. My ass could've played D1, yet there I was chasing down Daequan Cook's errant shots and wiping up Greg Oden's ball sweat. Screw that.

A few weeks after I tendered my resignation (if you know what I mean), I got a phone call from the same coach who originally promised me I'd be on the practice team (even though Ohio State has no such thing) and then completely failed to deliver on his promise. This time around he told me that a few players had gotten injured and, because of that, the team didn't even have enough guys to conduct a scrimmage in practice. I'll be damned if the next words out of his mouth weren't something about wanting to know if I would be willing to come back and serve as a practice player for the team.

Apparently he and Coach Matta remembered watching me play in a few AAU games when they were recruiting Greg, Mike, and Daequan, and they therefore had a solid understanding of what I could bring to the table. Still, I was hesitant to accept his offer since it felt a lot like déjà vu, but when he went on to say that I would actually be a walk-on and would get to sit on the bench during all the games, I decided it was a risk I was willing to take. When I walked into the players' locker room the next day and got ready for practice, Greg and Mike quickly figured out what was going on and came over to my locker to tell me how genuinely happy they were that I was on the team. Meanwhile, Daequan didn't say anything and most likely thought to himself, *Who the hell is this white boy?* even though he and I had been AAU roommates for years.

Once I was given a jersey and officially added to the roster, I felt a greater sense of power than I'd had when I was a manager. Sure going from manager to walk-on was only a step up in the college basketball hierarchy in the same way that going from Chris Kirkpatrick to Joey Fatone would be a step up in the *NSYNC hierarchy, but that didn't matter to me. This promotion gave me the confidence to say and do things that no other person in my position would ever have had the balls to say or do. Throw in the combination of me being a longtime friend of the best player on the team and also being fairly confident that Coach Matta and I shared the same sense of humor, and suddenly I felt untouchable.

In the next few days I threw some of my best jokes at Coach Matta to gauge how similar we really were, and he loved every one of them. From there, I made fun of a couple of my teammates in the locker room without any real consequence, either because they knew Greg had my back and could destroy all of them or because they were just laid-back guys. Either way, my confidence snowballed, and within a few weeks I had comfortably established myself as the comedic relief for our team. Coach Matta gave me the freedom to let me be myself, which was something I wanted so badly but was never allowed to do during high school, so I took the opportunity, ran with it, and made it the focal point of my four-year career at Ohio State.

So there you have it. That pretty much sums up how a guy from rural Indiana with no discernible talent not only found his way onto the number-one-ranked basketball team in America but also became one of the loudest voices (and unquestionably the biggest smart-ass) in the locker room of said team. As my time at Ohio State wore on and my "story" got more and more national exposure, high school kids from all over the country would often ask me for advice, usually because they planned to follow in my footsteps and emulate my career as a manager turned walk-on. While I'm always flattered that people think anything that comes out of my mouth is worth listening to, the truth is that it's really not that difficult to do what I did. All it takes is being born abnormally big, hitting puberty before everyone else your age, and taking a liking to basketball because you are so huge.

From there, you have to dominate local rec leagues to the point that refs feel the need to screw you over, and then consequently turn to AAU basketball in hopes of finding better competition. Next, make sure you play really well against one of the best AAU teams in the country (and make sure they're from the same city as you), and in the process expose a serious flaw of theirs that could be alleviated with your skill set. When they inevitably ask you to join their team, become good friends with your new teammate who just so happens to be the number-one recruit in America and pray that the NBA institutes a rule that makes guys go to college for at least one year before they enter the draft. After that, cross your fingers that your own basketball recruitment goes down in flames so you can follow your friend to whatever college he goes to and he can use his power as the team's best player to get you a manager gig.

Do your best to make sure the basketball team you are a manager for only has 11 guys on it, and then hope that a few of those guys get hurt so that maybe, just maybe, you'll be asked to join the team as a walk-on. From there, you're going to want to make sure that you can make fun of your teammates without getting curb-stomped, but not before you check to see if the head coach has a similar sense of humor as you and is one of the only college basketball coaches in America who would let you get away with screwing around on a daily basis. And that's really all it takes.

In other words, you have to be one lucky sumbitch.

PART TWO

MY BOY DAVE LIGHTY SAID WAS UP??????????? WHAT U THINK
ABOUT HIM CUZ HE SAID HE TRY N TO CHILL WITH U GET TO
KNO U. THIS IS DAVE LIGHTY BY THE WAY :) LOL

—Facebook message sent to a random girl
from David Lighty (my teammate from 2006 to 2010)
using my account

SEVEN

I was officially added to the Ohio State basketball roster exactly one day before the first game of the 2006–2007 season, which was pretty perfect for me since I was able to continue my streak of skipping preseason workouts that dated back to my freshman year of high school. When one of the assistant coaches called me on a Wednesday night and asked if I wanted to walk-on, I was actually in the middle of packing a suitcase because I had planned on leaving campus after my Thursday classes to go back home to Indiana for the weekend. My dad and I were also thinking of going to the Ohio State football game at Northwestern on that Saturday. Instead, I called my dad after I hung up with the assistant coach and told him that I wouldn't be able to go to the game or even make it home for the weekend because something had come up.

Being the parent of a kid he had just sent to college, he obviously assumed that "something has come up" meant that I either got arrested or got someone pregnant, or the opportunity had arisen to do things that could lead to getting arrested or getting

41

someone pregnant. Since the public perception seems to be that playing college basketball is synonymous with being in trouble with the law and/or fathering handfuls of kids, I guess he wasn't entirely wrong, but I still felt like I needed to assure him that I wasn't in any kind of trouble. When I told him that the assistant coach had asked me to walk-on (even though I had quit my job as manager two weeks earlier), he let out a relieved sigh and told me how happy he was for me. I can't say for sure, but I imagine my dad's turn of emotions was the exact opposite of what Laurence Fishburne felt when his daughter called to tell him that she had landed her dream job and then went on to explain that her dream job involved a bunch of random men putting their wieners in her cinnamon ring.

Shortly before practice started on Thursday, Coach Matta approached me in the practice gym and congratulated me before saying, "I hope you stayed in shape over the summer or you're going to be hurting the next few weeks." I assured him that I had been working out rigorously for the past few months and was in great shape, which was a claim that ranks right up there with "It's not you, it's me" and "I did not have sexual relations with that woman" on the list of the most blatant lies ever told. I'm pretty sure he could tell that I was lying (probably because I was 15 pounds overweight and had either barbecue sauce or Cheetos powder on every article of clothing I owned), but he nonetheless said okay and then started to walk away. After a few steps, though, he turned around and said, "I forgot to mention. Now that you're on the team, I'm going to have to ask you to shave your beard. It's nothing personal. Just a team rule."

As I told him that it wasn't a big deal because I actually planned on shaving it anyway and just hadn't gotten around to it yet, Greg walked by sporting a ferocious beard that made my beard look like Sidney Crosby's wispy excuse for facial hair. When I pointed to Greg with a confused look on my face, Coach Matta laughed and said, "Well, he's Greg Oden. You understand, right?" I shook my head in amazement at the blatant favoritism, laughed, walked to the court, started stretching for practice, and proceeded to ralph for the next two hours because I was so out of shape.

The next day was our first game of the season against VMI, and while Greg couldn't play because he was recovering from wrist surgery (he sat out our first seven games), Ohio State fans were obviously less concerned with Greg's wrist and more concerned with whether or not I'd be suiting up. That's because it was rumored throughout the day that there was a chance I couldn't play in the game since our equipment guy wasn't completely sure he'd get my jersey shipped from Nike in time, even though he had it express-delivered. Seriously.

I was all sorts of nervous, not only because I wanted to dress for the game but also because I knew it would be a huge letdown for my family to see me on the bench in street clothes after driving three hours to Columbus, not to mention driving themselves into a frenzy for the previous 48 hours over the thought of me playing college basketball for a Big Ten team. But in the end there was nothing to worry about because our equipment guy got the jersey from UPS in the early afternoon and finished stitching my name and number onto it with a few hours to spare (which I'm sure was much to the dismay of all the seventh-graders in attendance who were hoping he would be in such a hurry to get my jersey done that he'd forget to include the "U" in my last name). Crisis averted.

When the game finally started, it was the most mentally draining experience of my life. At any given moment, I was either pinching myself because I was living out a dream I'd had since I was five, or I was trying to get prepared to go in because I was naive and thought that Coach Matta might have been dumb enough to play me significant minutes for whatever reason. As I sat on the bench and watched us match VMI's up-tempo style of play, led by the nation's leading scorer in Reggie Williams (who now plays for the Charlotte Bobcats), my palms started sweating at the thought of possibly having to play. After all, the key to success against VMI is to have a team full of good ballhandlers in excellent physical condition (coincidentally, that's also the key to running a successful brothel), and those were two of my biggest weaknesses on a basketball court. In other words, the fact that disaster was inevitable was weighing heavily on my mind.

As the game progressed I realized that I wasn't going to see the court unless we got a big lead, thanks largely in part to an assistant coach telling me during a time-out, "You aren't going to see the court unless we get a big lead." This was originally a huge relief for me, but it didn't take long for us to build an insurmountable lead and make me start sweating bullets again. Then, with the game completely out of hand and only a few minutes left, Coach Matta finally gave me the nod and put me out of my misery.

I checked in with three minutes remaining, which was about 2 minutes and 45 seconds more than my body was physically prepared for, and said a quick prayer in which I asked God to not let me make an ass out of myself. Luckily, thanks to a little help from my adrenaline, the first two minutes went by in a flash. But when a VMI player shot a three in the last minute of play and the rebound fell into my hands, time seemed to stand still. I looked up to see a wide-open court ahead and did the only thing I thought made sense in that situation—I put my head down, started dribbling, and ran as fast as I could toward our basket. I didn't exactly have a plan, but since I was incredibly slow I knew I'd have plenty of time to figure it out.

Ultimately, I decided to try to score, most likely because I assumed the shot clock was about to run out after it took me an eternity to dribble down the court, and went up for a layup at the exact moment a VMI defender apparently wondered if he could shove his fist up my nose. I missed the layup, but since I was hammered, a foul was called and I was awarded two free throws. In that moment, I realized that I hadn't given the situation enough thought, as having thousands of people focus solely on me while I shot free throws was the last thing my battered nerves needed. But since I didn't have the wherewithal to fake an injury and let someone else shoot the free throws for me, I had no choice but to suck it up.

As the ref bounced me the ball, I told myself over and over, *Just don't airball it,* and did my best to deal with the sweat pouring from my palms. I took a deep breath, lined up the first shot, and let it go. What happened next is something I'll never forget. As luck would have it, the ball slipped right out of my hands as I released it, missed the basket entirely, and landed a foot short of the baseline.

Just kidding. I swished both of them bitches.

And with that, my illustrious college basketball career was off to a blazing start.

EIGHT

W e followed up our annihilation of VMI by beating Loyola Chicago and Kent State in consecutive days to win the BCA (Black Coaches and Administrators) Classic, which really wasn't that big of a deal because everybody knows the BCA Classic is only three-fifths as prestigious a tournament as the WCA Classic. Nonetheless, winning the tournament was important to the guys on our team because, even though we had only played three games and all of our opponents were less than stellar, rattling off three straight wins with ease seemed to confirm our collective initial thought that we had a chance to be pretty special. After all, the chemistry we showed on the court was nothing more than an extension of the great team chemistry we had already established off the court.

The first time we all took notice of how well we worked together was at "The World's Largest Pillow Fight," which is an event held on Ohio State's campus at the start of every academic year that has never once actually set the record as the world's largest pillow fight. Because of the nature of the pillow fight, most of us saw this as our first team-building test, and if that is in fact what it was, there's no denying that we passed with flying colors. And by "passed with flying colors" I obviously mean that everyone on the basketball team and I (I hadn't been added to the team yet) picked out a couple of nerds, ganged up on them, and beat them senseless to the point that we probably could have been arrested for attempted murder.

Sure it was alarming that to Jamar Butler, who once cracked the windshield of his own car when he punched it in a sudden fit of rage, a "pillow fight" apparently meant "wrap a tiny pillow around your knuckles and punch people in the face." And sure it was probably not great for society that a bunch of big, strong athletes (and me) basically brutally assaulted a handful of defenseless kids, but you know what? I'm willing to look past all of that because what really mattered was that we assaulted those kids *as a team*. When Jamar noticed that Daequan was having trouble making a kid's face bleed, he showed Daequan that he had his back by connecting a vicious right hook to the kid's schnoz. And when Jamar failed to knock another nerd completely unconscious, Daequan returned the favor and put the kid's lights out. Meanwhile, I filled in wherever I could and used my Ultimate Warrior Wrestling Buddy to blindside as many people as possible. It was the kind of teamwork that would have made any coach proud. And just so we're clear, what I wrote in this paragraph is only a slight exaggeration of what actually happened.

Since Coach Matta made all the basketball players live on the same floor of the same dorm (upperclassmen included), we basically spent every second of every day together, which made it that much easier for us to build our chemistry even more. (This also made things a lot easier for the groupies, since they could just move one room over after their services were no longer needed in the original room they visited.) This might come as a surprise to some, but because we were athletes, Ohio State hooked us up and put us in a dorm that typically housed graduate students, which is to say that it wasn't like all the other dorms on campus in that every unit had its own bathroom, kitchen, and living room to go along with the bedroom. The upperclassmen were given individual units, but the freshmen weren't as lucky. The four freshmen who were actually recruited to play basketball at OSU all shared the same kitchen and living room, but their dorm came with two bathrooms and each guy got his own bedroom.

I, on the other hand, was at the bottom of the totem pole and therefore had to share every room with my roommate, who, like me, was also a longtime friend of Greg and Mike and had used his relationship with them to become a manager for the basketball team. (Our dorm was still better than what every other freshman had on campus, so I can't complain too much.) Anyway, because the four other freshmen all had full-ride scholarships and essentially were given unlimited money from the school to spend on food, and I was a walk-on who had to pay for everything out of my (parents') own pocket, I developed a Robin Hood mentality and frequently raided their fridge and food pantry whenever they were gone. (For reasons still unknown to me, they never locked their door when they left.) Looking back, I have no idea why I kept trying to swipe food from them when all they usually ever had in their dorm was orange soda, Sour Skittles, and hot sauce, but I guess that just goes to show how dire my financial situation really was.

After a few months of stealing food that I didn't even like, I got a pleasant surprise when I found over half of a large pizza in the fridge one day, figured that would be my dinner for the evening, and decided to take the entire box back to my room. (Yeah, I know stealing food like that is a dick move, but I rationalized it by convincing myself that I was pulling a prank on them. It made sense to me at the time.) But as I took a few steps out of the kitchen and toward their front door, Greg came out of his bedroom and caught me red-handed. Before I could utter a word, he turned back to his room and yelled, "Aw hell naw! You're a dead man!" I looked down at the box, saw Greg's name written on it, and instantly realized he was going back to his room to get his Nerf gun. Yes, you read that right—his Nerf gun.

You see, Greg carried this Nerf gun with him pretty much everywhere he went and would shoot guys on the team with it whenever he felt we were out of line. He thought of himself as the leader of our team and felt it was his duty to keep everyone under control, which he apparently thought could best be accomplished with help from a children's toy. The "bullets" of the gun were Styrofoam darts with suction cups attached to the ends, but after Greg got drunk with power and started shooting people for no reason in particular, it got annoying real fast.

Anybody who has a son or has babysat a toddler boy knows what I'm talking about. Sure it doesn't hurt, but it only takes one instance of having a dart suctioned to your forehead because Greg/ the toddler came out of nowhere and shot you in the face while you were trying to watch TV for that damn Nerf gun to piss you off. Well, I reached my boiling point with him and his Nerf gun when that exact thing happened to me. He quickly figured out how much I hated that thing and decided to annoy me with it even more. (I would've done the exact same thing if I were him, so I can't really blame him.) The Nerf gun was my nemesis and he knew it. This is why I had no doubt in my mind what he was doing when he headed back to his room.

I shot out of their dorm with pizza in hand and Greg and his Nerf gun on my heels. As I was running down the hallway back to my room, I dropped the pizza on the floor for no other reason than I was trying to use the same strategy that those bad guys use in movies when they create an obstacle/diversion by tipping over trash cans as the cops are chasing them through an alley. This was a terrible idea and in no way worked like I thought it would. Undaunted, I continued my sprint toward my dorm, busted open my door, and made a beeline for my bathroom. After months of regularly eating whatever it was Ohio State's cafeterias tried to pass off as food, this was a procedure I had rehearsed many times before, and all that practice helped me gain a little ground on Greg.

Right as Greg followed my trail and came through the front door of my dorm, I stepped into the bathroom and slammed the door shut behind me to lock him out.

In an act of desperation, Greg shot a dart at me before I could get the door all the way closed, but he missed and the dart ended up in the bathroom with me. I knew Greg wouldn't mind waiting it out, and I knew as soon as I opened the bathroom door I'd be faced with a barrage of darts, so it was clear to me that my only way out was to do something so drastic it would cause a ceasefire. In other words, my only choice was to suction that dart I had with me to my nuts.

I unzipped the fly of my jeans and let my boys breathe, and then put a little water on the suction cup of the dart to make it stick to my sack. With my nads hanging out of the fly of my jeans and the dart solidly latched onto them, I opened the door and told Greg if he wanted his dart back he'd have to grab it himself. He was so appalled at the sight of one of his darts fastened to my junk that he lowered his gun and admitted defeat. And with that, I had achieved the impossible: I killed Greg's desire to use his beloved Nerf gun.

After I eventually removed the dart and put my testes back in my pants, Greg and I laughed off the incident and watched some TV. Five minutes later, when whatever show we were watching went to commercial, Greg grabbed his Nerf gun and asked, "How many darts do you think I can get stuck to the TV?" I told him there was no way he could get five of the six darts to stick on the TV screen because the suction cups on the darts didn't work very well, to which he simply replied, "You're on."

He gathered all of his darts, made them all point the same direction, bunched them up in his fist, and ran his tongue over each and every one of them to improve their suction. I decided to wait for him to finishing licking the darts before I reminded him that one of them had just been attached to my scrotum, and once I did, he tried to convince me that that particular dart wasn't in his hand. But when he looked down and saw that he was holding all six darts, he realized that he couldn't deny the truth any longer.

Greg dropped the darts in horror and disgust, stormed out of my room, and never once tried to shoot me with his Nerf gun again after that. As great as my initial victory was, the fact that he took it to another level by licking the dart that was attached to my scrotum made the victory that much sweeter (which is funny because judging from the look on Greg's face, my nutsack was actually really, really salty).

What that story has to do with the team chemistry concept I was originally talking about in this chapter I'm not sure, but does it really matter? Greg Oden indirectly licked my balls. Don't act like you won't think about this story every time someone brings up Greg's name in conversation or you see him on TV, which was pretty much my only motivation in telling the story in the first place. Besides, the prank war that was ignited between us shortly thereafter had to have helped our team chemistry somehow, even if it was entirely one-sided and basically consisted of me being a dick by putting a bunch of packing peanuts under his bedsheets or hiding an alarm clock set for 4:00 a.m. in his room and him not really retaliating at all. (Some would argue that he was just being nice, but I subscribe to the theory that he wasn't creative enough to think of any good ways to get me back—either that or he was too busy being the most dominant center in college basketball in over a decade.)

Nonetheless, whether Mike was in my room playing me in H-O-R-S-E on the little goal attached to my door, or Kyle Madsen was begging me to do his math homework for him, or Daequan, Jamar, and Ivan Harris were trying to get me to serve as the judge in their debate concerning who "gets with the baddest bitches," there was always something going on at the dorm to keep me entertained. And while it got exhausting at times to have to be around the same people all day every day, I'm glad we all lived on the same floor because I seriously do think that our team's collective camaraderie was that much better because of it.

NINE

Following our domination of the BCA Classic, we took care
of business in home games against Eastern Kentucky and
the two-time national champion San Francisco Dons, who
everyone knows as the alma mater of NBA great Bill Russell but
very few people know as the alma mater of NBA not-as-great Bill
Cartwright. After playing the Dons, our next game was against
Youngstown State, which I thought was an interesting coincidence
considering that a "don" is obviously a mob boss and Youngstown
is sometimes affectionately referred to as "Murdertown, USA"
because of its history of car bombings orchestrated by the Mafia.
So there was that. Anyway, the game was played at Nationwide
Arena in downtown Columbus because our on-campus arena was
probably hosting a Hanson concert or something else much more
important than a college basketball game.

Luckily, this didn't affect fan attendance all that much—there
was still a great turnout for the game, if for no other reason than
that, after years of futility from the Columbus Bluejackets, the people of Columbus were finally excited to actually see a good local

team play in Nationwide Arena. Either way, the game was a complete blowout and was pretty much over from the start, which is to say that I knew before the game that I had a pretty good chance of playing. And I was right.

With a minute left and us up by about 30, I checked into the game and did a quick stretch to help prevent my ice-cold hamstrings from exploding. Since I had played in a handful of games before this one and, as you know, already had two career points to my name, I wasn't nervous this time around and was instead actually pretty excited to get in the game because, after missing my first career three-point attempt in the San Francisco game, I was anxious to redeem myself and get my first three under my belt. I wasted no time doing just that.

Following a missed shot by Youngstown State just a few seconds after I checked in, I put my head down and sprinted back toward our basket to spot up by the three-point line. But before I could get completely set, Jamar threw a pass to me while I was in midstride and messed up my rhythm. Instead of making the smart basketball decision and collecting myself before shooting, I was so desperate to score that I just caught the ball, turned my body toward the rim, and let a shot fly, all in one motion, even though I didn't really know how far away I was from the goal until right as the ball was leaving my hands. That ultimately didn't matter because, by some act of God, I made it. When the ball went through the rim, the crowd went crazy and my adrenaline took over as I sprinted back on defense because I was so excited.

After I got situated on defense, though, I looked into the stands and noticed that of the 17,000 people who were there for the first half, maybe a couple thousand had stuck around until the end of the game. What's worse, I realized that the only reason the people cheered so loudly when I scored was because they thought it was cute in a Jason McElwain sort of way that someone as bad as me could actually put the ball in the basket instead of tripping over his own feet like they expected. Needless to say, I wasn't exactly thrilled with the over-the-top cheering, but there wasn't much I could do about it. The fact of the matter was that I really *wasn't* anything but a novelty human victory cigar to Ohio State fans, and that was just the way it was going to be for the rest of my career. I can't overstate how big of a wake-up call this was for me, as it reshaped how I viewed my role as walk-on for the rest of my four-year career.

After my three polished off our dismantling of Youngstown State, we took our show on the road for the first time and played sixth-ranked North Carolina in Chapel Hill. Even though we had vaulted to a number-one ranking shortly after the Youngstown State game, North Carolina was actually favored, not only because they were playing at home, but also because our star center was out with a wrist injury while their star center, Tyler Hansbrough, was the Tim Tebow of college basketball (which is my way of saying that he was portrayed as the greatest college basketball player of all time in the history of the world ever).

Heading into the game, everyone knew this would be our first big test of the season, including Coach Matta, which is why he organized an impromptu film session the night before the game. Now, our typical routine was to watch film the night before every game, so that part wasn't unusual, but when a few managers knocked on our hotel room doors and told us to meet in a conference room downstairs for film in five minutes, we could sense a sincerity surrounding this film session that wasn't there when we prepared for our first six games.

When we walked into the conference room, we were greeted with dim lights and a blank projector screen surrounded by all of the coaches. Once the players got situated, Coach Matta stood up and with a serious look on his face said, "I don't need to tell you how big tomorrow's game is. This is no doubt a great test for this basketball team, but you gotta believe me when I tell you that the game will be won between the ears. Understanding what North Carolina is going to try to do is essential to our success, so pay attention and don't be afraid to ask questions." He then sat down and pushed Play while the rest of us focused our attention on the screen.

Instead of clips of North Carolina, though, the projector showed the legendary meatloaf scene from *Wedding Crashers*, when Owen Wilson's character meets Will Ferrell's character, Chaz, at Chaz's house. Being the huge Will Ferrell fan that he is, Coach Matta thought that showing this clip would be an effective way to keep the team loose, and judging from the fact that the entire room burst into laughter when Will Ferrell stepped out from the shadows with nunchucks around his neck and said, "What the fuck do you want?" to Owen Wilson, I'd say that he got exactly what he was after. (Yes, we watched actual game tape of UNC after that.)

Fast-forward to the next night when, ten minutes before the tip-off, our team gathered in the locker room for one last pep talk. This meeting typically never lasted much longer than a couple minutes and usually consisted of Coach Matta going over strategy one last time before saying a few encouraging words to get us pumped up. But this time around we sat silently in the locker room without having any idea where Coach Matta even was.

With less than five minutes until tip-off, the door opened and Coach Matta slowly walked in holding each end of the towel that he had draped around his neck. He calmly made his way to the front of the room, stood pat, and only moved when he turned his head to look each and every player square in the eye. While I can't speak for everyone, I can say that the serious look on Coach Matta's face made me more than a little nervous about what he was going to do.

Finally, after a few beats of silence, Coach Matta finished staring down all the players and opened his mouth for the first time to say, "What the fuck do you want?" in the exact tone Will Ferrell used in *Wedding Crashers*. The entire locker room lost it. To this day I think this was Coach Matta's finest moment in coaching. After the laughter subsided, he just said, "All I want from you guys tonight is to just go out there and have fun. All right, now bring it in for the real thing."

It was quite possibly the greatest pregame speech in the history of coaching and no doubt helped calm the nerves of our freshman-laden team. And even though we ultimately came up a little short and lost the game by nine, pretty much every college basketball fan around the country agreed that giving the sixth-ranked team a run for their money on their home court without our best player was a sign that we were going to be a team to be reckoned with once we got Greg back.

TEN

Despite initially being told that he wouldn't be able to play until January 1, Greg was given the okay by team doctors a month early and made his debut in our next game against Valparaiso on December 2. As bad as this news was for Valpo players and fans, it was good news for Kyle Madsen, who had transferred to Ohio State from Vanderbilt in the off-season and was relatively shy and timid because he was still trying to figure out how he fit in with his new teammates. Since he had just transferred and was therefore ineligible to play for the entire season per NCAA rules, Kyle had been given the assignment of playing Greg one-on-one on the side court every day in practice until Greg was cleared to scrimmage with the rest of the team, which was a role that basically just consisted of Kyle getting violently (and often hilariously) dunked on over and over again. So when Greg finally healed up and led us to an easy victory against Valpo, and consequently let Kyle off the hook for the rest of the season, well, I guess you could say Kyle was slightly pleased.

After Valpo, we rattled off three more blowout wins against Cleveland State, Cincinnati, and Iowa State to improve our record to 10–1. While all three of these games were largely uneventful, I'd be remiss if I didn't mention that the Cincinnati game was played just a few miles from my hometown right outside of Indianapolis and, even though I got to play in the final minute, the block of people from my hometown who had been chanting my name all night didn't get the chance to see me do anything of any importance on the court because the other walk-on on our team, Danny Peters, followed in Daequan's AAU footsteps by airballing a shot instead of passing it to me. (Consider this my retribution, Danny.) But alas, we got the win and that's all that matters (or whatever other cliché phrase athletes use when they're secretly pissed at a teammate but don't want the public to know). In fact, that win and the victory over Iowa State gave us four straight wins and helped us climb back up to third in the polls, setting up a top-five matchup in our next game against the fourth-ranked defending national champion Florida Gators.

Leading up to the game at Florida, neither the college basketball experts around the country nor Doug Gottlieb had any idea of what to expect. We had obviously shown that we were a very talented team, but there was no denying that Greg wasn't yet back to full strength, which raised a lot of question marks. Meanwhile, Florida was the defending national champion with pretty much everyone back, but leading up to the game their star center, Al Horford, had been battling a sore ankle, which had brought his effectiveness into question too. Seemingly no one could make a confident prediction about who would win, but despite all of the unknowns surrounding the game, the one thing everybody could agree on was that this was the game of the year in college basketball up to that point.

For 23 minutes, it was everything everyone expected it to be. After being down by nine at halftime, we put together a nice comeback to knot the game at 40 with 17 minutes left to play. But then

Florida suddenly kicked it into high gear, beat us like we were an NFL wife, and consequently made the game a bigger letdown than *Saved by the Bell: The College Years*. When it was all said and done, we had lost by 26 points, which was such an ugly beat-down that I could've sworn I heard Digger Phelps describe it on ESPN later that night as an "ass raping." I still have no explanation for our monumental collapse, mostly because everything happened in such a blur that I can barely remember anything from that game. And by that I clearly mean that I stopped paying attention when we got down by 10 and decided to check out Florida's cheerleaders for the rest of the game instead.

We took our frustration out on Coppin State a week after the Florida loss by beating them by 37 points in what was our last nonconference cupcake game. I checked into the game with two minutes left and, with the Youngstown State game fresh in my mind, decided I wasn't going to shoot no matter how open I was. This almost proved to be a disastrous decision when, following a Coppin State miss, one of my teammates secured the rebound and threw a pass down the court to me, as I was running back toward our basket, and in doing so triggered a fast break that I had total control over yet wanted no part of.

Not really knowing what I should do, I took a few dribbles toward the basket as the Ohio State fans all yelled "Shoooooooot!" in unison, and for a second I came *this close* to giving in to their request. But when I got to the three-point line and picked up my dribble to go up for a shot, the lone Coppin State defender who had been back on defense during the entire sequence ran toward me to challenge my shot. As this happened, I saw out of the corner of my eye what appeared to be a black guy in a white jersey streaking toward the basket and instinctively made the decision to just throw the ball up toward the rim and hope like hell whoever I was throwing it to could complete the alley-oop. What I failed to notice, though, was a second defender trailing behind my teammate. As the ball left my hands the defender caught up to my teammate and jumped in the air to steal my pass, but through some sort of divine intervention, he was a little too late and slapped Dave Lighty on the arm right as Dave caught the pass and stuffed it through the rim.

I was stunned. Not only did Dave finish the alley-oop, but he got fouled in the process, which made it that much more of an impressive play. Plus, the fact that I had blindly thrown the pass without having any idea of who I was throwing it to, let alone whether or not he was expecting me to throw him an oop, made it even more insane that it actually worked out. Throw in the fact that I had never in my life had one of my alley-oop passes completed with a dunk (and the last time I had tried was when I launched a pass over the backboard in an attempt to set up Daequan during an AAU game), and it's nothing short of a miracle that the play resulted in anything but crippling embarrassment. Anyway, that single play will forever be the proudest moment of my athletic career, which is to say that when I have my midlife crisis in 20 years, I'm almost certainly going to force my future kids to watch this play thousands of times while I repeatedly say to them, "Look how good Daddy was."

Conference play started after the Coppin State game, and we opened with a win at home against Indiana and a win at Illinois, running our record to 13–2. Up next for us was another marquee matchup, this time against fourth-ranked Wisconsin in Madison, yet virtually nobody in Ohio cared because the Ohio State football team had lost to Florida in the BCS Championship the night before and at Ohio State vandalizing cars and setting couches on fire in response to a football loss (and a win for that matter) takes precedence over everything else.

Still, after losing our first two big road games of the year, everyone on the team agreed that this game would be a good barometer for us, even though we had no idea that a barometer is an instrument used by scientists to measure atmospheric pressure and in no way measures how well a basketball team is currently playing. Anyway, we were dealt a serious blow the day before the game when Danny contracted mono and was told by the team doctor that he wouldn't be able to make the trip to Madison. This was upsetting news, not because Danny contributed anything to our team (he didn't), or because I genuinely cared about Danny's health and well-being (I didn't), but rather because Danny and I were roommates and his absence meant I had to now share a hotel room with Ivan Harris until Danny got healthy. (I'll explain why this was so bad in a second.)

With a shorthanded bench thanks to Danny's illness, we ended up losing by three in a hard-fought game that saw us down by as many as 20 in the second half. It was encouraging to see us claw our way back into the game after folding in a similar situation against Florida, but it was almost more painful to ride the emotional roller coaster of coming so close to pulling off a comeback but ultimately falling short than it was to just simply get blown out. Plus, to make matters worse, Wisconsin's cheerleaders were butt ugly.

After the Wisconsin loss dropped our record to 13–3, we went on a tear and rattled off 22 straight wins, beginning with a squeaker over 20th-ranked Tennessee at home. Since the game was played on a Saturday, we stayed in an on-campus hotel the night before, which was standard procedure for us on weekend games because Coach Matta is a firm believer in limiting the players' opportunities to do stupid things that could make them play poorly the next day. As previously mentioned, I was given the honor of sharing a hotel room with Ivan because Danny's mono still had him out of commission, which was something I dreaded due to the fact that Ivan and I couldn't possibly have been more different people. At Wisconsin, I avoided having to hang out with Ivan by just going straight to bed when I got back to my room after watching the National Championship football game in another room, and since that strategy worked so well the first time I thought I'd try it again. I hung out in the room of one of my other teammates for most of the night, and when I eventually got tired I returned to my room and got ready for bed right away.

While I got situated in my bed and tried to fall asleep, Ivan mostly kept to himself and only spoke every few minutes when he'd let out the occasional "daaaaaammmmn" in reaction to whatever he was watching on his laptop. (There's a 0 percent chance it was anything other than basketball highlight videos or porn.) Despite these random outbursts, I eventually fell asleep, but after five minutes of shut-eye I woke up in a puddle of sweat (yet another reason why I missed Danny as a roommate—white guys like the room a little chilly, but the black guys prefer a sauna). Desperate to cool down, I decided my only hope was to sleep naked, so I took my pants off, tossed them to the side of my bed, and pulled my sheets up over my body so my junk wasn't out in the open. This proved to be a great decision, because my body temperature quickly dropped to a normal level and I almost instantly fell back asleep. A couple of hours later, though, I was woken up again, this time by a faint female voice in the room. I popped my head up, squinted my eyes in the direction of the voice, and saw Ivan and the mystery girl whispering to each other next to Ivan's bed. I then looked toward the end of my bed and was greeted with the sight of my own bare ass staring back at me.

Apparently I had gotten hot again while I was sleeping and brushed the sheets to the side of the bed in the middle of my slumber without even knowing it, which was a technique that worked wonders for me when I slept in my own bedroom by myself. The obvious problem, though, was that I wasn't in the room by myself this time around. Because the lights to our room were on, it was almost a certainty that the girl Ivan brought into the room saw my exposed, pale, and hairy rear end. What's worse, since I sleep on my stomach and usually spread out to take up the whole bed, there's a good chance she also could see between my legs and got a decent glimpse of my man meat too.

Being as naive as I was, I felt a sense of embarrassment come over me at the thought of accidentally showing my private parts to Ivan's sister or cousin or whatever relative it was he was talking to.

I quickly covered myself back up and tried my hardest to fall back asleep and avoid the awkwardness.

A few minutes passed before the lights were turned off and I heard the door close, leading me to believe that Ivan's relative had left and he was finally going to go to bed. Right as I was dozing off, I heard Ivan softly say something and assumed he was talking to me since I was still under the impression that I was the only one in the room. When I rolled over to see what he wanted, though, I clearly heard Ivan say, "Oh yeah, girl. Work it just like that," and realized what was going on. Ivan was lying in his bed, holding his sheets up, and looking underneath said sheets to watch the performance. That's right—Ivan was getting a beej as I lay awake ten feet from him.

To say I was stunned would be a bigger understatement than saying the temple guards from *Legends of the Hidden Temple* had pedophiliac tendencies. Even more disturbing was that, after seeing me roll over in my bed, Ivan turned his head my way, looked me in the eye, raised his eyebrows, and stuck out his tongue as if to say to me, "She's putting my penis in her mouth! Isn't this awesome?!" I rolled back over in my bed and distinctly remember thinking to myself that nothing in the world could have possibly made me feel any more uncomfortable.

Following the Tennessee win, nothing too crazy happened either on the court or off the court for the rest of the regular season, which is my way of saying that I didn't play in very many games and I didn't attach any Nerf darts to my scrotum or witness one of my teammates get orally pleasured. But truth be told, we did have a handful of exciting games after our thriller against Tennessee, the first of these being a home win against Michigan State at the tail end of January in which we led by 20 at halftime but almost choked it away thanks to Drew Neitzel dropping 24 points on us in the second half.

The next close call was at Penn State, where we again relinquished a big lead and only won by two despite being on the verge of a blowout earlier in the game. We were especially lucky to win this game because Penn State's best shooter, Mike Walker, missed a wide-open three at the buzzer that would've won them the game and surely would have been the greatest moment in Penn State basketball history. Hell, come to think of it, it's still probably the greatest moment in Penn State basketball history that he even had an open shot to beat the number-one team in the country in the first place.

Either way, we had our rematch against Wisconsin 11 days later in what was the first Big Ten game to ever feature the number-one team in the country against the second-ranked team in the country. (We were first in one poll, and Wisconsin was first in the other, so it technically was the first-ever Big Ten matchup of two top-ranked teams.) Thanks to a last-second shot by Mike, we won the game by one and clinched the Big Ten regular-season championship, but stuff that happens on the court and doesn't involve me doing my best to avoid embarrassing myself is boring and can be read about in a bunch of other books, so let's just move on.

Our last regular-season game of the year was at Michigan, and since we had already clinched the Big Ten championship and were basically guaranteed a top seed in the NCAA Tournament, we really didn't have much to play for. Michigan, on the other hand, had everything to play for, as both their NCAA Tournament hopes and the job security of their head coach, Tommy Amaker, rested solely on our game. This was the primary reason why they gave us a run for the money and kept it close, but we went on a 10–0 run to finish the game and won by four, Michigan went to the NIT, and Tommy Amaker was fired after the season. Suck it, Michigan.

After closing out the regular season, we played Michigan again in the first round of the Big Ten Tournament in Chicago and again had our way with them. Then we beat Purdue for the third time in the season in the semifinals, setting up the grudge match with Wisconsin in the championship. But as thrilling as the first two games against the Buzzcuts were (I refer to Wisconsin as the Buzzcuts because 99 percent of the guys who have played for Bo Ryan at UW have had buzzcuts—look it up, it's a fact), the championship game was anticlimactic as we steamrolled them en route to a 23-point win that was never really anything to sweat over.

I actually got to play in the final minute and made the most of my time by setting up the biggest what-if play of my career. In my first defensive possession of the game, the guy I was guarding caught the ball on the wing, and I let him dribble around me (at least that's what I tell people) so I could do that poke-from-behind steal that pretty much every white guy who has ever played basketball has gotten good at since it's usually our only hope on defense. I knocked the ball out of the Wisconsin guy's hands and took off running toward the other end of the floor as the ball fell right into Danny's lap. (Danny had finally finished his bout with mono by that time.)

See if you can guess what happened next. Your two choices are that either (a) Danny saw that I was wide open and had at least a 15-foot head start on all the guys on Wisconsin, threw the ball up to me, and I completed the only dunk of my college career, or (b) Danny covered up the ball to ensure that he properly secured it, slowly dribbled up the court, and then proceeded to miss a layup in traffic to cap off an offensive possession in which Danny was the only guy on our team who touched the ball. Here's a hint: the answer is "b." So to recap, just a few months after freezing me out in my hometown, Danny stripped me of a legitimate chance to dunk in the Big Ten Tournament Championship.

For those who doubt whether I actually would've been able to dunk had Danny passed to me, consider this: the only time I ever dunked in a game in my life was in eighth grade, when I used the exact same "poke-from-behind steal and take off running" strategy that I used against the Buzzcuts, only in eighth grade my teammate passed the ball up ahead to me. (Yes, I seriously dunked in eighth grade—I tried to tell you earlier that I was a monster when I was younger.) So yeah, if I could've completed the same play in eighth grade, I don't think I would've had much of a problem as a college freshman. Nonetheless, I think the saddest part of this whole situation is that, even though Danny repeatedly cockblocked me on the court throughout the season, I *still* would have much rather shared a hotel room with him than have to suffer rooming with Ivan again.

ELEVEN

Winning the Big Ten Tournament improved our record to 30–3, which was good enough for us to get a number-one seed in the NCAA Tournament for just the third time in program history. We drew Central Connecticut State for our first-round game that was to be played at legendary Rupp Arena in Lexington, Kentucky. Even though I had played in almost half of the games up to that point, I was pretty nervous about this game because the NCAA Tournament is a completely different beast, and since Central Connecticut State kinda sucked I figured there was a good chance I'd get to play. And once again, I was right. We jumped all over Central Connecticut State right out of the gate and never looked back, giving me an opportunity to make my lifelong dream of playing in the NCAA Tournament a reality.

When Coach Matta gave me the nod with a minute left, I tried to mentally approach the game as if it were any other, which is to say that I told myself over and over not to try to do anything special and to instead just do my best to stay out of the way. But no matter how hard I tried to convince myself it was just another game, I couldn't calm my nerves. After all, I usually only played in front of a few thousand people, but because this was a tournament and there was another game after ours, the fans from the other two teams had combined with the Ohio State fans and the 12 Central Connecticut State fans to pack Rupp Arena. Throw in the fact that millions were watching on TV and my attempt to convince myself it was just another game was a lost cause.

As I walked to the scorer's table to check into the game, Coach Matta could tell I was nervous, so he stood up from his chair and called me over to him. He then put his hand on my shoulder, looked me in the eye, and waited a second before he said, "Don't fuck this up," and returned to his seat. Pretty sound advice, really. With these four words resonating throughout my head, I calmed down enough to grab a rebound and outlet the ball to Danny after my first defensive possession of the game. Then my built-up karma was put to good use when Danny took a couple dribbles and tried to throw an alley-oop to Ivan from half-court but threw it too high and consequently made himself and Ivan both look bad. Justice never felt so good.

Our second-round game was against Xavier, where Coach Matta had coached three years earlier before he decided to ditch them and come to Ohio State. Naturally, Xavier fans lost their minds over having to play their former coach and booed and heckled him the entire game for being a traitor, as if they honestly expected him to stay at a program that had had one Sweet Sixteen appearance before he got there, paid him less than half of what he now makes at Ohio State, and had no ties to him until he coached there for three years. Still, the history surrounding Coach Matta gave the game an "upset in the making" feel to it. Simply put, Xavier wanted to beat us, and they wanted to beat us badly.

And for the first 37 minutes, it showed. They had total control over the game and took a nine-point lead into the final three minutes thanks to their big guys being able to step out and knock down threes on a consistent basis, which is really a necessity for any mid-major team trying to pull off an upset. But heading into the final media time-out, we decided that it would probably be better for our National Championship hopes if we won the game instead of letting Xavier continue to outplay us.

We turned up our intensity and cut the lead to just one with a minute and a half still left to play, but try as we might, we couldn't get over the hump and take the lead, or even tie the game for that matter. When Jamar's attempt to put us ahead with 18 seconds left went begging, and Dave's shot after he grabbed the offensive rebound also missed, things looked bleak. (I distinctly remember sitting on the bench trying to figure out where I was going to go for spring break the next week since I figured we wouldn't be playing in the tournament anymore.)

Xavier secured the rebound after Dave's miss, and Greg fouled the guy who had the ball with only nine seconds left to play and us still down by two. Xavier only needed to make two free throws to ice the game and send us back to Columbus with our tail between our legs. But they only made the first one, leaving the door open for one last desperation shot to send the game to overtime. Ivan secured the rebound after the second free throw and gave it to Mike, who then dribbled up the court with the clock winding down to under five seconds and . . . wait, why am I telling you this? You already know what happened. And if you don't, shame on you.

(All right, I guess that was cold of me to leave those of you who don't know what happened hanging, and to strip Ron Lewis of his moment of glory that comes with being mentioned in my book. If you must know, Mike handed the ball off to Ron, who then made what has to be the biggest shot in Ohio State basketball history by hitting a deep three with a hand in his face that sent the game to overtime. From there, Mike took over by scoring 11 points in OT, and we won by seven. In case you are undecided about whether or not you should look up Ron's shot on YouTube, I feel obligated to mention that Gus Johnson called the game. So yeah, put the book down and go watch the video if you haven't seen it before.)

Beating Xavier earned us a trip to the Sweet Sixteen in San Antonio, where our first game was a rematch with Tennessee. My first priority upon arrival was obviously to find Pee-wee's bike in the basement of the Alamo, but I had no luck and gave up after an hour of looking for a basement that I'm not even sure exists. Anyway, when I eventually checked into our hotel on the River Walk, I realized that this road trip would be my favorite of the year. That's because when I walked into my room I saw a door toward the back that was cracked open, decided to take a peek behind it, and was greeted by the "El Gobernador" suite on the other side, which in Spanish means "the most badass hotel room I've ever seen in my life."

Apparently the maid forgot to lock the door leading to the suite, which meant Danny and I had access to a full kitchen, a dining room, a living room, a walkout balcony that overlooked the River Walk, and another bathroom to go along with the standard room we originally had. In other words—and this is what's really important here—I didn't have to room with Danny anymore. It goes without saying that I left our original room for Danny and took over the suite for the week (I slept on the pullout couch in the living room). And even though every time that I left the room I had to figure out a way to disguise from the maid that the door to the suite was unlocked, it was completely worth it because I ~~could order porn off the hotel TV for free since the hotel management was under the impression the suite was empty and therefore wouldn't know who to charge~~ had an awesome view from the walkout balcony.

Our game against Tennessee was the second of a doubleheader at the Alamodome, with the first game being a matchup between Memphis and Texas A&M. (The winner of our game was to play the winner of that game to go to the Final Four.) We got to the arena about an hour before we could even take the floor for warm-ups, but because Coach Matta wanted us to focus on Tennessee and not look ahead to who we would play in the next game, we hung out in the locker room for that time instead of sitting in the stands to watch the other game. At some point while we were waiting, Coach Matta and Ivan had to use the restroom at the same time and ended up peeing next to each other in adjacent urinals.

According to Coach Matta, while they were peeing, the 25,000+ people in the arena burst into a furious roar that shook our locker room, presumably because Texas A&M made a good play. (Since we played in San Antonio, there were more A&M fans there than the other three teams' fans combined.) As the story goes, when Ivan heard the thunderous cheers, he turned to Coach Matta and asked, "What's going on out there?" to which Coach Matta replied, "I don't know for sure, but I think it's a high school wrestling match or something." Ivan responded with, "Oh, that's cool," finished his business, and walked away without giving even half a thought to how ridiculous it would be for a Sweet Sixteen NCAA Tournament game to be held up by a high school wrestling match, let alone that there would be that many fans going crazy over high school wrestling. But as much as I like to make fun of Ivan, I have to give him credit on this one—he took Coach Matta's words to heart and avoided looking ahead to our next game, even if it was because he was the perfect combination of oblivious and just plain dumb.

Right from the start, Tennessee came out of the gates like a bat out of hell and we came out like Rex Ryan trying to get up off the toilet. They jumped all over us and had a comfortable lead that ballooned to as many as 20 points before dipping down to 17 by halftime. Strangely, nobody on the team (except me) was really that discouraged when we got to the locker room during the break, probably because Ron's heroics the game before proved that a comeback was entirely plausible. Still, even with Ron's shot fresh in our minds, there seemed to be a weird confidence in the locker room that was largely unwarranted since, ya know, we had just gotten blown out for the first 20 minutes of the game.

It almost felt like the guys who actually played all got together before the game and decided they'd suck in the first half just for the hell of it and see if they could pull off a comeback in the second half. Now that it was halftime they all had that "everything is going according to plan" look on their faces, while I sat in the back of the locker room scratching my head as to what exactly that plan was and whether or not they knew we were up against a seemingly insurmountable lead. But they apparently knew what they were doing because we came out in the second half with fire in our eyes and murder on our minds. In just a little over 10 minutes, we erased their entire 17-point halftime lead and tied the game, prompting Coach Matta to give his famous "Their assholes are tight!" speech during a time-out, which is a speech that he always gives when we have a team against the ropes and basically just consists of him yelling "Their assholes are tight!" over and over.

As it turned out, Coach Matta's speech may have been a little premature because Tennessee's assholes, in fact, weren't *that* tight. They gathered their composure and had an answer for just about everything we threw at them for the last eight minutes. But with the game tied and six seconds left on the clock, Mike went for the jugular as he took the ball to the hole and drew a foul to put him on the free throw line to all but win the game. He made the first free throw but missed the second, giving Tennessee one last chance.

Tennessee's Ramar Smith secured the rebound and raced down the court, and Bruce Pearl chose to play out the final seconds instead of calling time-out to draw a play up. With Mike on his hip most of the way, Smith took the ball the length of the court and threw up a layup as the buzzer sounded—only to have Greg fly out of nowhere and send his shot into the bleachers. And with that, we completed one of the best comebacks in tournament history and set the record for the biggest halftime deficit overcome to win an NCAA Tournament game in regulation time.

As entertaining as the second half was, the best part of the game came just after Greg's block, when everyone on our bench stormed the court in celebration and I ran straight to Greg and gave him a bear hug (I was probably just trying to get on TV). He wanted no part of it, though, and made me look like the world's biggest doucher by disregarding me like I was a condom and he was Shawn Kemp. I know I just asked you to look up Ron's shot against Xavier on YouTube, but I'm now *demanding* that you put the book down to find and watch the video of my fat face and terrible haircut giving Greg a hug. Those few seconds of hilarity are a perfect representation of every walk-on–star player relationship ever and provide a rare glimpse of my douchey early days as a walk-on before I stopped caring altogether and became unfathomably lazy.

Our second thrilling win over Tennessee of the season gave us the right to play Memphis—who also happened to win their game in exciting fashion—for a trip to the Final Four. Leading up to the game, Memphis's center and dumb-ass extraordinaire, Joey Dorsey, told the media that he had been looking forward to playing against Greg for a while because Greg was "overrated" and "might be as good as Joey Dorsey." Sadly, neither of those quotes claimed the title as the dumbest thing he said before the game. That's because he also went on to say, "It's going to be David and Goliath. I'm Goliath. He's the little man. I'm going to outwork him to every ball. I think I'm going to have like a 20-rebound night." Yes, you read that right, and yes, that is a direct quote.

Never mind the fact that Dorsey had the audacity to call out a First Team All-American and make it seem as though Greg should be honored to be in the same sentence as him. No, the real genius lay in the fact that he chose to label himself as Goliath in his analogy, proving that either he had never actually read the story of David and Goliath or he was too dumb to see the irony in identifying with a giant whose overconfidence and perceived sense of invincibility ultimately led to his demise. As you might have guessed, Dorsey's prediction turned out to be halfway correct. Sure he completely whiffed on predicting that he'd grab 20 rebounds and get to every loose ball, but his David and Goliath analysis was spot-on. When it was all said and done, Joey "Goliath" Dorsey finished the game with more fouls (four) than points, rebounds, assists, blocked shots, steals, and IQ points combined (three rebounds, zero of everything else). Meanwhile, Greg "David" Oden put his handful of stones and his slingshot to good use by leading us to a 16-point victory with 17 points and 9 rebounds, and in doing so helped us earn the first Final Four trip for Ohio State since ~~1999~~ 1968. (Coincidentally, "a handful of stones and a slingshot" is just one of the many nicknames Greg used to have for his genitals.)

TWELVE

I f I had to describe the Final Four in only thirteen words, this is what I'd say: it's essentially just a weeklong circus with a few basketball games thrown in. We arrived in Atlanta four or five days before our first game against Georgetown because there were all sorts of practices, banquets, meetings, and media commitments we had to tend to before the game. But even though all of the hoopla got annoying pretty quickly, I never got sick of the media sessions held in our locker room every day before and after our practices.

Since I was a freshman walk-on and was therefore entirely unknown, nobody in the media ever wanted to interview me, which is to say that I had nothing but free time during these sessions. And it goes without saying that I used this free time to do everything in my power to distract my teammates as they were getting interviewed. The way I saw it, no teammate and no method of distraction was off-limits.

My favorite move was to stand behind the interviewer and violently thrust my hips with a goofy look on my face (think of Ace

Ventura in front of all the cops after he solved the Roger Podacter murder case), but every now and then I'd throw in a Happy Gilmore "riding the bull" dance just to mix things up. When reporters would swarm around Greg and shove their tape recorders in his face, I'd grab my cell phone, join the cluster, and make it my goal to see if I could get close enough to actually have my phone touch Greg's face.

The crowning achievement of my interview-distracting career was no doubt when I stood behind a guy interviewing Ivan on TV and tried to show Ivan that he had a booger hanging out of his nose. This went on for a few minutes until Ivan eventually saw me out of the corner of his eye and said to the interviewer, "We're just going to go out and play our game and . . . hold up—do I have a booger in my nose? Hang on a sec. I gotta go to the bathroom real quick and take care of this."

It may seem like I was an ass for distracting my teammates, but the truth is that everyone on the team pulled pranks on one another all throughout the year, so by the time the Final Four came around, doing things like distracting teammates during interviews was pretty common among our team. Besides, I got my fair share of pranks pulled on me, it's just that I'm purposely choosing not to write about them because I refuse to give my teammates the satisfaction of knowing their prank on me was successful. Anyway, the point is that it was all good-natured because we were an extremely close-knit group of guys who genuinely loved being around one another, which is something that can't be said about other Ohio State teams I was on (more on this in later chapters). This camaraderie wasn't limited to just the players, though, as many of our coaches also felt a strong bond with our team and weren't afraid to have some fun with us.

Perhaps the best example of this happened at one of our open practices at the Georgia Dome. We were forced to have open practices at every stop in the NCAA Tournament, but at the Final Four these practices generated a lot more fan interest and were more for show than they were during the first few rounds of the tournament.

Since it was basically just an exhibition for the fans, Coach Matta, who was mic'd up by ESPN, decided not to show too much from a strategic or conceptual standpoint and let us just shoot around the entire time. Midway through the practice, he walked over to me, covered the microphone that was clipped on his shirt, and told me he wanted to have some fun. He said, "I like to think that there's some guy in a trailer outside the arena right now closely listening to everything I'm saying. Let's confuse the hell out of him."

This sounded like a great idea, so I told him I'd play along with anything he said. A few minutes later, Coach Matta called my name.

"What's up, Coach?" I asked as I approached him.

He put his arm around me. "Listen, Mark, we've already established that you're our secret weapon and we're gonna play you at least 30 minutes on Saturday. But if you keep shooting this badly, I'll have no choice but to play Oden over you. I mean, I've watched your last 10 shots and I honestly can't tell if you're trying to shoot a basketball through a basket or if you're trying to put your dick in your own ass. Well, I got news for you. You gotta pull your head out of your ass before you can put your dick in there. Now get your shit together, go back out there, and make a shot."

Is that exactly what he said? Probably not. But he definitely hinted at a plan to play me most of the game instead of Greg, he said something that didn't make a whole lot of sense to me, he cursed a lot, and he calmly scolded me for being terrible. So that's close enough. Either way, I remember verbatim what he said when practice was over and all the players gathered around him for his standard post-practice talk.

After we all congregated at half-court and waited for him to share his thoughts on how practice went or whatever else he had on his mind, Coach Matta (still mic'd up) stepped into the middle of the group and said with a straight face, "All right, guys, let's go ahead and start our usual post-practice routine. Everyone drop your drawers to your ankles and let's get this circle-jerk going."

THIRTEEN

By the time our game against Georgetown rolled around, nobody on our team seriously thought we had any chance of losing. Georgetown was good and had a handful of solid players (led by Jeff Green and Roy Hibbert, who now play for the Boston Celtics and Indiana Pacers, respectively), but they were methodical on offensive and we were confident that we understood their system well enough to stifle them. Heading into the game, all the focus was on the matchup between Greg and Hibbert because both guys were seven-footers who could defensively dominate the game, but Greg picked up two fouls in the first three minutes and sat on the bench for pretty much the entire first half. It wasn't looking good for us early on, but the rest of the guys on the team stepped up, and we took a four-point lead into halftime.

The second half played out a lot like the first, with the big exception being that Greg was back on the floor. To be honest, most of the game was pretty boring to me because of the combination of Georgetown's style of play and the fact that I never once thought we could possibly lose. Thankfully, though, Greg made things exciting for a brief moment in time when he trailed a fast break, caught a pass from Jamar as he was steamrolling his way toward the basket, and proceeded to execute the greatest missed dunk I have ever seen in my life. Greg caught the ball just inside the free throw line, collected himself, jumped from about six feet away from the basket, and tried to put his testicles in Jeff Green's mouth as his head rose above the rim.

It was such an impressive missed dunk that Ohio State fans still use the picture of Greg at his apex with our entire bench rising in anticipation as their computer background picture or their Facebook picture, which suggests that they've decided to reject reality and just pretend that he actually made the dunk. (It should be noted that although Greg missed, a foul was called on Jeff Green.) Anyway, other than that missed dunk and the fact that it put us in the National Championship for a shot at redemption against Florida, there isn't much I remember about that game.

Heading into our rematch with Florida, I had a weird sense of confidence. They were the defending national champions, they had beaten us earlier in the year by 26, and they were led by the greatest women's basketball player of all time in Joakim Noah, but for some reason I honestly thought we had a legitimate chance to win because they would be overconfident or something. During the pregame warm-up, though, my confidence quickly vanished thanks to Daequan. While the rest of the team was getting prepared for the biggest game of their lives, I stood on the sideline to let the real players have enough room to do whatever it was they had to do to get ready. Daequan noticed me standing off to the side and decided to come talk to me instead of focusing all of his attention toward warming up, because of course he did.

"Well, Bru," he said (he always called me "Bru" or "Brutus" because he thought I looked like Ohio State's mascot—whatever that means), "looks like this is going to be our last game together." After being teammates for the previous five years, I took this statement as Daequan's way of telling me that he was going to go to the NBA instead of returning to Ohio State for his sophomore year.

Forget the fact that I thought it was a bad decision for him to leave early. I was more concerned with him telling me about his decision 10 minutes before the National Championship game was set to tip off, which was a pretty good sign that he didn't have his priorities lined up all that well.

It's okay, though, because he surprised everyone and played out of his mind once the game started. Wait, never mind. He actually scored two points and only played nine minutes because he screwed up on so many inbounds plays that his mental errors directly led to 10 Florida points and Coach Matta couldn't risk playing him any more after that. Sorry about that mix-up.

Other than Daequan not being mentally prepared for the game, the other fatal mistake our team made was Coach Matta's decision to keep me on the bench. You see, right after the starting lineups were announced, I approached Coach Matta and explained to him that I had five fouls to give and they'd go to waste if I didn't use them, so if he should need me to go in and violently foul Joakim Noah or Al Horford, just to send a message, I was more than ready. I mean, Temple coach John Chaney used this strategy against St. Joe's in 2005 (when he infamously referred to his player as a "goon"—which makes it sound like the kid should've been playing for the Monstars), so it wouldn't have been a completely unprecedented move. Nonetheless, Coach Matta just laughed and told me he'd "keep that in mind." But here's the thing: he didn't keep it in mind. At all. In fact, I'm pretty sure he had his mind made up all along that he wasn't going to play me. I'm not saying that this is why we lost, but then again, I'm not saying it's not.

After we lost by nine in a hard-fought game, I walked off the court with a hanging head as orange and blue confetti fell from the rafters and thousands of Florida fans did their Gator Chomp. We came so close to achieving something I had dreamed about my entire life, but we were stopped short by a team featuring a guy whose ponytail looked like a wad of pubes. It was, without a doubt, the most demoralizing feeling of my life.

As I took one last look at the throngs of Gator fans cheering, I couldn't help but think that our season wasn't supposed to end this way. It felt like I was watching a terrible finish to an otherwise great sports movie. Like if Jimmy Chitwood airballed what would have been the game-winning shot, fell into a deep depression, and died a week later on his bedroom floor with an empty bottle of painkillers in one hand and a half-full bottle of Jack in the other. Or if the Giants were destroyed by the Cowboys in *The Little Giants* because Icebox realized she wasn't a lesbian and decided to stay on the cheerleading team. Or if Rudy didn't get to play in the last game because he was mouth-raped by the team captain in an act of hazing and decided to quit a month before.

Yeah, that's exactly what it felt like.

I walked into the locker room, sat next to my locker, put my chin on my chest, and thought about what just happened. Everyone else on our team pretty much did the same thing. The collective mood was as somber as could be, and the silence was deafening. Coach Matta made the first move and gave a quick speech about how he had no regrets about the game, about how much he'd miss coaching our team, and how he'd remember that season for the rest of his life. We all "brought it in" and did that obligatory "team on three" thing that every sports team in the world does, then went back to sitting by our lockers in silence. Even though Coach Matta insisted that we "keep our heads up," nobody was interested in what he had to say. This wasn't a time for reflection. It was a time for pouting.

The mood was so dismal that when I looked to my immediate right I noticed Danny had started to tear up. Under any other circumstances, he would have been berated by everyone on the team, but the truth is that we all felt like crying that night, even if our tears didn't actually materialize. For most of us, losing the National Championship wasn't what was so upsetting. No, what really made us so emotional was knowing that, because of graduation and a few guys leaving early for the NBA, our close-knit group would never get to all play together or regularly hang out ever again. Every one of us had the time of our lives that season, and now it had all come to an end. And so, we all just sat still, blankly stared at nothing in particular, and felt sorry for ourselves.

Even when the coaches and staff left the locker room, we remained frozen next to our lockers, unsure of when or if the time would come where we would feel like getting up. After what felt like an eternity, Greg saw Danny crying from across the room and stood up from his chair. As the leader of our team and really the only reason our game with Florida was relatively close, Greg apparently felt obligated to come talk to Danny to try to console him. He walked toward Danny and me with the same dejected look on his face that all of us had. When he reached us, he pulled up a chair, sat next to Danny, and put his arm around him. Then he said something to Danny that is the best advice I've ever heard in my life:

"It's only a game. Stop crying like a little bitch."

In the end, Florida was one of the best college basketball teams ever and was certainly the best team in the past 15 years, so it's hard to get too upset about the loss now. But in that moment, I'd never been more upset about something that didn't involve death or my junior high girlfriend refusing to show me her boobs. Not only had we come so close to achieving a dream, but now our season was over and consequently the brotherhood we all had was pretty much over, not to mention the fact that I'm pretty confident our team would've easily won the National Championship in just about any other year. Wow, never mind—I guess that really is depressing to still think about. Let's just move on.

About a week after we lost the National Championship, we held a rally for Ohio State fans at our arena that looked back on one of the best seasons of Ohio State basketball ever and gave people a chance to say good-bye to Greg and the seniors (and, of course, Daequan). Even though everyone had a pretty good idea that Greg was going to go to the NBA, Ohio State fans figured it was at least worth a shot to try to persuade him to stay. As the team was introduced, the few thousand people in the stands burst into a "One more year!" chant that drowned out whatever was being said by whoever had the microphone. Once the chanting subsided, the interview portion of the rally started, with Danny and me as the first players interviewed.

Ohio State basketball legends Bill Hosket and Ronnie Stokes conducted the interview, and since the entire thing was scripted, I knew going in that these two guys were just going to toss us one or two questions so they could quickly get to interviewing the good players without making us feel left out. Hosket said, "Both of you guys started the season in a unique way, as team managers. And then obviously became an integral part of this basketball team." I still can't tell if this was meant to be a joke—for his sake, I hope it was. "Tell us a little bit about that transition."

Danny and I had already planned for me to field the first question, so I leaned into the microphone and went for it: "First I'd just like to make an announcement real quick. I hear the fans chanting, 'One more year,' and I just wanted everyone to know that after sitting down with my family . . . we've decided that I'll be back next year!"

I stood up and waved to the crowd as they ripped into a perfect combination of applause and laughter for 10 to 15 seconds. The next day all sorts of articles appeared online and in our local newspaper about the pep rally, and I was the focal point of seemingly every one of them. Everywhere I went for the next week I was recognized as that basketball walk-on who said he'd be coming back for his sophomore season. My announcement received infinitely more attention than I ever anticipated it would, and the people of Columbus and the Ohio State fans were eating it up.

And just like that, my "legend" was born.

PART THREE

*I was going to vote (in the 2008 presidential election),
but it was raining and I was wearing new Jordans.*

—Danny Peters, my teammate from 2006 to 2010

FOURTEEN

I don't mean to come across as a philosophical hippie or something, but I like to think that the world is a perfectly balanced place that always finds a way to restore its balance should it ever be disturbed. The way I see it, just about everything in life has a built-in punishment for when things are taken too far and enjoyed in excess. In other words, with respect to Daryle Singletary, I actually do believe it's possible to have too much fun and bad things happen when that "fun threshold" is reached. (By the way, if you are one of the nine people who got that Daryle Singletary reference, pat yourself on the back for being such a die-hard fan of the greatest genre of music of all time—'90s country.)

For example, if you eat too much, you'll get fat. If you have too much sex, you'll most likely get an STD or an unwanted pregnancy. If you drink too much alcohol, you'll either vomit or go home with a fugly chick that you'll regret in the morning. And if you are attracted to a girl just a little too much, and you stand in the shrubs just outside of her house with your pants at your ankles and watch her every move through her living room window, you'll most likely go to jail or at the very least get a restraining order slapped on you. (Some chicks just can't appreciate a true gentlemanly gesture.)

In my case, I was having too much fun with basketball. In my first year of college, I lucked my way onto a Big Ten basketball team, I lucked my way into a scholarship (I forgot to mention that the basketball program had extra full-ride scholarships, so they gave me one that would've otherwise gone to waste), and I lucked my way into a front-row seat to one of the more thrilling NCAA Tournament runs in history that culminated in a trip to the Final Four and a shot at the National Championship.

In a single season I had been able to do things that most people—even most *Division I basketball players*—would never have the opportunity to do. Quite simply, things were too good to be true for me, and my world needed to balance itself out and somehow bring me back down to earth. But, you might be asking, with the exception of being kicked off the team, what could possibly bring you down from the high that must have came from going to the Final Four with your childhood friends? Answer: Evan "The Villain" Turner, that's what.

After my magical freshman season ended with us coming up just a little short against Florida in the National Championship, the only three guys at Ohio State I had known before I enrolled at the school (Greg, Mike, and Daequan) all chose to forgo their final three years of eligibility and enter the NBA draft. For Mike and Greg, this was a pretty obvious decision—the "draft stock" for both guys was as high as it was ever going to be after they both played out of their minds throughout the NCAA Tournament. And while I originally thought that Daequan, who was our sixth man and averaged only 10 points per game, was crazy for leaving early, I changed my mind after I found in his dorm a five-page paper he had written for a class that had a big red "0%" at the top of it and a note from his professor on the back page that read, "It's obvious that you didn't read the book and had no understanding of what was expected with this assignment. Your entire paper discusses things that are irrelevant for this assignment and this class. Please come to my office sometime this week."

I still can't believe the professor dropped the ball on a perfect opportunity to quote *Billy Madison*: "What you have just written is one of the most insanely idiotic things I have ever read. At no point in your rambling, incoherent response were you even close to anything that could be considered a rational thought. Everyone in the English department is now dumber for having read it. I award you no points, and may God have mercy on your soul." But I digress. What I'm trying to say here is, Daequan wasn't exactly suited for higher education and it was probably a good idea for him to enter the workforce as soon as he possibly could.

When those guys left, not only did I lose a few friends, but I also lost my security blanket. I was comfortable busting my teammates' balls throughout my freshman year because I was friends with the two best players on the team and figured that was enough to get me a free pass. In no way was this true (I got a "free pass" because my teammates were laid back), but it didn't matter because that's how I thought. So when those three guys left, I initially kept to myself and tried to figure out how I fit in with my new team.

The combination of isolating myself in the locker room, being the only guy on the team who didn't live in the dorm (I had a one-bedroom apartment five miles off campus), and being kind of antisocial to begin with took its toll. Instead of going out with some of the guys on the team after practices, most nights I'd lock myself in my apartment, stare into a mirror, and remind myself that I was a loser with no friends. (I wish I was joking.) After a few months of this, my mom finally got through to me and convinced me to try to "start being yourself again." I gave her advice some thought and realized she was right—I needed to go back to doing the things that made my freshman year so awesome, even if my old friends weren't around anymore. Thus, the next day at practice I went back to being my old self by finding ways to pick on the freshmen on our team, which was a group that included a guy by the name of Evan Turner.

Other than Evan, the freshmen on our team during my sopho-more season were Jon Diebler, Dallas Lauderdale, Kosta Koufos, and Eric Wallace. And while I made fun of every one of them pretty much every day, Evan was by far my favorite target because he made it incredibly easy to get under his skin. When I made fun of Jon for looking like McLovin and being pigeon-toed, he laughed about it and made fun of me for having a muffin top. When I made fun of Dallas for wearing a neon-green undershirt with a brown hoodie for a week straight, he took it as a compliment. When I made fun of Kosta for sticking his chest out and looking at himself in the mirror when we lifted weights, well, he didn't pay attention to me because he was too busy sticking his chest out and looking at himself in the mirror. And when I made fun of Eric for being even more socially awkward than I was, he wouldn't say anything and would just smile and give me a high-five before walking away.

None of those guys ever got too worked up over anything I said because they knew it was just all in good fun. But Evan was different. How was he different, you ask? Put it this way: you know how after your Little League baseball games everyone would ride in the back of a pickup truck to Dairy Queen and your coach would deliver bad news by telling you that you were only allowed to spend two dollars each? If you answered no, I weep for your deprived childhood. But if you answered yes, you surely remem-ber how the cool kids would pool their money together and get a Treatzza Pizza that they'd split three ways. And how the not as cool yet still perfectly normal kids would just get an ice cream cone, a couple of Dilly Bars, or a Peanut Buster Parfait, or whatever. Well, Evan was like that one doucher little kid in the group who spent his money on a Mr. f'ingMisty and a small order of fries. I trust you now have a solid understanding of just how weird Evan was.

When Evan came to Ohio State, he had a huge chip on his shoulder and his mind made up that everyone was trying to either piss him off or keep him from playing in the NBA. In his defense, I eventually did make it my goal to try to piss him off every day, but that wasn't until a couple years later, so there was no real excuse for his initial paranoia. But whatever the case, from the moment he set foot on campus he was the epitome of a guy who couldn't take a joke.

So when I decided that it was time for me to "start being myself again," Evan didn't take too kindly to any jokes I made at his expense. Being the asshole that I am, I took his reactions as an open invitation to make him a target until he learned to lighten up and realize that his teammates had his back and wanted the team to be just as successful as he did. This only added fuel to fire and led to Evan and me becoming sworn enemies. We butted heads for the better part of three years, and by the time our tenure as teammates was eventually through, Evan had tried to fight me no less than three times and actually threw punches on one of those occasions.

FIFTEEN

I f you were to ask any of the guys on the 2007–2008 Ohio State men's basketball team what the feeling in the locker room was like in the months leading up to the start of the season, my guess is that every one of them would tell you that an obvious schism existed. (Okay, so most of the guys probably wouldn't know what "schism" means and would've just described the locker room as a nonviolent version of the East Coast–West Coast rap feud or the Bloods and Crips, but you get the idea.) The year before we had successfully integrated a high-profile group of freshman recruits with the veterans of the team, but this time around was a different story. Because of our run to the National Championship game, the new crop of freshmen felt a sense of entitlement and expected to be the focal point of the team and just cruise to the Final Four like the freshmen before them had. This immaturity offended us older guys, and we took pride in putting them in their place when they refused to acknowledge that we knew more about what it takes to win in college basketball than they did.

Perhaps the most telling sign that we couldn't work together as a team was when we returned to The World's Largest Pillow Fight at the start of the school year. Instead of obliterating our undersized classmates like the year before, we were overpowered to the point that Kyle was hit in the face so hard with a pillow by some random kid that one of his eyes literally watered for the next 72 hours. It was obvious that leadership was sorely lacking, and as a sophomore walk-on, I didn't feel I was in a position to step up and bring the team together, so I just sat back and watched the madness unfold.

The coaches eventually picked up on the rift and organized a trip to a local SWAT team obstacle course just a few weeks before practice was set to start as a way to help with the team-building process. This obstacle course was used by the real Columbus SWAT team for their training and consisted of running, jumping, ziplining, climbing, crawling, push-ups, pull-ups, sit-ups, and all sorts of other things I was terrible at, which kind of made me wonder if the coaches were trying to run me off the team. I should mention that compounding the problem of me being unathletic and a little overweight was the fact that I had swollen testicles because I was still recovering from a surgery I had over the summer to fix a varicocele in my sack. And by "I should mention," I mean that I should keep that information to myself because it's incredibly personal and embarrassing, and writing about it in my book is proof that I obviously have no self-respect.

Nonetheless, even though my nutsack was honest to God the size of a softball, my urologist had cleared me for physical activity because he claimed that I had fully healed from my surgery. (He and I clearly had different definitions of "fully healed.") Since swollen balls apparently weren't a legitimate excuse to sit out, I had no choice but to suck it up and do my best to get through the obstacle course, which I found out right away would be more challenging than I could have ever anticipated.

When we arrived at the SWAT facility, a group of cops greeted us and told us to split into two teams for a competition to see who could get through the obstacle course the quickest. Now, common sense would say we should have mixed the teams up so that freshmen and veterans were both on each team, which explains why we did the exact opposite. One group was comprised of the seven guys who had been on the team the year before, while the other group was made up of the six new guys.

The veterans decided to go first so we could set the tone and then taunt the younger guys as they went through the course, and we also decided that our weakest guy (from the standpoint of who would take the longest to get through the course) should start us off so the stronger guys could clip his heels and motivate him to move faster. As you could probably guess, thanks to the shot put in my pants, I was that guy.

"The first thing you gotta do," one cop said as he pointed to a 20-foot log suspended eight feet in the air, "is climb up onto that and shift your way across. If you're strong enough, just hang off the side and move across it like you would on monkey bars. If you've got good enough balance, you can run across it. But if you lose your grip or fall off, you've got to start over. That's why pretty much all of us agree that the best method is to straddle it and just scoot backwards the entire way." Seeing as how I wasn't strong and I had terrible balance, this meant my only choice was to use the straddling method. With a ballsack the size of an orange. Awesome.

After what seemed like 30 minutes of scooting and sarcastically yelling "I ain't no bitch!" for no reason in particular, I ended the most painful experience of my life and made it across the log. Once I conquered that first obstacle, the rest of the course was a breeze, which is to say that the rest of the course didn't directly involve me putting a ton of pressure on my swollen testicles as I dragged them across a log. In the end, even though we had to overcome my genital problem and we had one more person in our group, the veterans still beat the new guys by over 10 minutes, which led to trash-talking by both groups and only made matters worse. By the time we all made it back to our gym, showered, and went home, the veterans and new guys probably had more animosity for each other than when the day started. So yeah, I'd say the whole team-building thing kinda backfired.

A couple of weeks later, we played our first exhibition game against Ashland on Halloween night and won by 29, which gave us all sorts of false confidence. After all, just one season earlier we had played in the Division I National Championship game while Ashland went 16–12 in Division II, so there really wasn't any reason for us to be pounding our chests. Our overconfidence came back to bite us in the second and final exhibition of the season a week later against Findlay, when the combination of thinking we were better than what we actually were and the increasing lack of unity on our team made the game a memorable one for all the wrong reasons.

Although, like Ashland, Findlay was a Division II team, they had gone 28–5 the year before and had most of their team back, making them the favorites to win the D-II National Championship that year (which they ultimately did en route to a 36–0 season). But our guys apparently thought all D-II teams were created equal and didn't see Findlay as a serious threat. This proved to be a terrible decision because Findlay and their slew of upperclassmen ended up beating our mess of a team by two points on our home court. So to recap, seven months after coming within one game of being crowned the best team in Division I college basketball, we suddenly weren't even the best team in Division II.

Needless to say, Coach Matta was less than thrilled with the loss and called for a 6:00 a.m. practice the next morning, which consisted of an hour and a half straight of nothing but one-on-one defensive drills (his biggest gripe with the Findlay game was our inability to guard the guy with the ball) and was, without a doubt, the most miserable practice of my life at any level of any sport. After the practice, I crawled my way back to the locker room and fell asleep in my locker as I angrily thought about how dysfunctional our team was. When it hit me that we still had yet to even play a real game, I realized that there was very little chance that this season was going to be anything but a thoroughly entertaining train wreck.

SIXTEEN

F ollowing the embarrassing loss to Findlay, Coach Matta's message sent via the 6:00 a.m. practice came in loud and clear, and we played pretty well in our season opener against Green Bay. We were expected to destroy Green Bay, so it wasn't anything to brag about, but it was a win nonetheless, and with the team we had that year it was hard to say just how frequently we'd have the opportunity to celebrate wins. We followed that up with a win over Columbia the next night to earn a trip to Madison Square Garden for the final two rounds of the preseason NIT. Our first game in New York City was against Syracuse on the Wednesday before Thanksgiving, but we got to the city on Monday because there was a banquet being held for the four teams left in the tournament. (Texas A&M and Washington were the other two teams.)

The only reason I even bring this banquet up is because it was organized by ESPN and Dick's Sporting Goods: ESPN was to televise the remaining games of the tournament, and Dick's was the chief corporate sponsor of the preseason NIT. Why was this important? Well, it was customary with these tournaments for the corporate sponsor to provide some sort of gift for the players involved, and we found out at the end of the night that our gift was a bag from Dick's filled with handfuls of stuff, including a gift card to their store. And because ESPN was also involved, St. John's coach Steve Lavin, who worked as a commentator for ESPN at the time, was the emcee for the banquet and was therefore responsible for informing us about our gift bags.

After dinner, Lavin approached the podium for his closing remarks or whatever and ended his speech by saying, "I almost forgot to mention that Dick's has graciously provided a little goodie bag for all the players. So, before you leave, don't forget to stop by the table back there and pick up your bag of Dick's . . . stuff." Nobody knew whether he was trying to make a joke or whether he just picked a bad time in the sentence to catch his breath, so a few people let out some light chuckles while the rest of us did our best to hold our laughter in. But then Lavin made matters worse when he followed it up with "There's a lot of good stuff in there that I think you're going to be excited about, especially if you like Dick's."

At this point, most people assumed he was purposely saying these things, and a small roar of laughter erupted through the room that muffled out Lavin's final "good luck to all the teams and good-night everybody" comments. To this day, I'm still bothered by whether or not Lavin knew what he was saying. In fact, screw wanting to know who really shot JFK—if I could get one question answered about an event throughout the history of the world, it would definitely be "Was Steve Lavin purposely making dick puns at the 2007 preseason NIT banquet, or was it just a hilarious coincidence?"

After we got back to our hotel in Times Square and exhausted all the Dick's jokes we could think of, we turned our focus on Syracuse. We were unranked, but Syracuse was 21st in the nation and playing close to home, so we had a good opportunity to get a statement win of sorts. And despite all the chemistry problems we had, we were able to do just that. We controlled most of the game and ended up beating Syracuse by 14 points, thanks in large part to

Kosta Koufos having a breakthrough game with 24 points and 9 rebounds. But as much as Kosta (who now plays in the NBA for the Denver Nuggets) would've liked to have all of us tell him how great he was, the truth was that most of the guys actually resented his successful game because his ball-hogging on the court and immature social skills off it had already helped earn him the title of team douche bag.

A few weeks earlier, at a house party on Ohio State's campus, Kosta spent the entire night either lecturing us about why we shouldn't drink beer or awkwardly trying to high-five every girl who walked by us. He was so intolerable that after hours of following everyone around and explaining how beer "makes you fat" and "kills your brain," one of our senior captains, Matt Terwilliger—the one guy who could beat up everyone else on our team—finally shut him up in awesome fashion by pouring an entire beer on Kosta's head while Kosta was in midsentence. Then, just a few weeks after the Syracuse game, Kosta started his season-long trend of standing up in the middle of the time-out huddles so he could neglect what Coach Matta was trying to tell him and instead talk to his mom in the stands. (Sadly, I'm not kidding.)

Throw in the fact that he was a colossal ball-hog for most of the season and that he basically hijacked the Ohio State basketball program for a year to help himself get to the NBA, and it's easy to see why Kosta was a complete outcast on our team. So when he shot 4 for 16 in a blowout loss to Texas A&M in the championship game of the tournament and then never again played as well as he did against Syracuse, well, I guess you could say that more than a few guys on the team were pleased. More than anything else, this active cheering against a teammate by most of the guys on the team tells you all you really need to know about how dysfunctional our team was that season.

We got back on the right track after the Texas A&M massacre by beating VMI at home pretty handily, but turned right around after that game and lost a tough one at home to second-ranked North Carolina. What made that particular loss so frustrating was that we played pretty well in the first half and were up by three at halftime, but went ice-cold in the second half and squandered a close one. What made it even more frustrating was that we did pretty much the exact same thing in our next game at 16th-ranked Butler, where we led by as many as 14 in the first half but collapsed down the stretch and lost by 19.

Losing to Butler just a few miles from my hometown was bad enough, but getting manhandled in the second half after dominating the first half for the second straight game was an inexcusable embarrassment. I had no choice but to suck it up, though, and take the jabs about the loss from my friends in Indiana because for the past six months or so I had obviously been taking credit for our trip to the Final Four and it was only fair for me to accept the blame for defeat if I was going to expect praise for the victories. Whatever the case, what was really important was that for the first time in my brief college basketball career my team had suffered two straight losses. Seven games into the season, our record was 4–3, with three of those wins coming against teams that I could've played serious minutes for (which meant those games didn't really count for anything). Things were looking bleak.

SEVENTEEN

With some help from a relatively weak stretch in our schedule, we responded well to Ohio State basketball's first losing streak in almost three years by going on an eight-game winning streak. It started with a 47–39 win over Coppin State at home that was every bit as boring as you'd think and was described by the AP as a game "played at a glacial pace." After that, we blew out the Presbyterian Blue Hose, who clearly have the best nickname of any school in college basketball. The Presbyterian game was a significant one because it marked the last time I did anything of any importance on the basketball court and therefore served as the end of the serious side of my college basketball career.

I checked into the game with one minute left, and thanks to a huge misunderstanding, I was not only passed the ball but I was also provided with a ball screen from Kyle. You see, after I hit the three in the Youngstown State game my freshman year and embarrassingly got treated like J-Mac by the fans, I vowed then and there to never shoot during a game again. I tried explaining this to my teammates many times, but I apparently never got through to them because every time I stepped on the court at the end of games, they would pass me the ball and try to get me an open shot so I could score. (Now that I think about it, there's a good chance they did it only because I repeatedly asked them to do the exact opposite.) Anyway, Kyle set a screen to get me open, either because he thought he was doing me a favor or he was intentionally trying to annoy me, and I had no choice but to use his screen and take a couple dribbles toward the top of the key.

As this happened, the court opened up, but I felt a defender a couple steps behind me. Unsure of what to do, I decided to shot-fake to make it look like I was trying to make a legitimate basketball move . . . even though in truth I was hoping it would give the defender enough time to catch up, which in turn would eliminate any chance of me shooting the ball. Unfortunately, the opposite happened. He bit on my shot-fake, flew through the air, and left me wide open. At this point, I had no choice but to let the shot fly and hope for the best, which is obviously another way of saying I confidently shot the three, smoothly sank that bitch like it was nothing, and then backpedaled all the way back on defense like a motherf'ing boss.

Following our win over Presbyterian, we beat Cleveland State in Cleveland by 17 to set up a National Championship rematch against Florida in Columbus. Even though both of our teams were completely different (Jamar was the only returning starter for either team) and were nowhere near as relevant on a national scale, the handful of veteran guys on our team desperately wanted some measure of revenge, no matter how small. And based on the fact that 19,000 people packed our arena and made the atmosphere more electric than Blanka in "Street Fighter II," I'd say Ohio State fans wanted some revenge as well.

But as hungry for payback as we were, nobody wanted to beat Florida more than Coach Matta. That's because, from what I've been told, when Florida coach Billy Donovan and Coach Matta met at half-court to shake hands and wish each other good luck right before the tip of the 2007 National Championship, Donovan apparently said to Matta, "Don't worry, Thad. I lost the National Championship game the first time I got here too." So when we took over the game with about eight minutes left in the first half and never looked back on our way to a 13-point win, it was no surprise to me that Coach Matta led the celebration in the locker room as if we had won some sort of championship and not just another regular-season game.

We followed up the big win against Florida (that really wasn't that big of a win since we were playing at home and Florida kinda sucked) with a high-scoring victory over Maryland–Baltimore County, a road win against a bad Illinois team, and a couple of home wins against an awful Iowa team and an even worse Northwestern team. With a 12–3 overall record, we were in a tie for first place in the Big Ten with a 3–0 conference record and were feeling pretty good about ourselves.

But sadly, the good times didn't last much longer as another second-half collapse in a road loss to Purdue in our next game triggered our descent into mediocrity for the rest of the season. We dropped our next two after that to eleventh-ranked Michigan State and seventh-ranked Tennessee, and while both losses were relatively close and came on the road against highly ranked teams, the bottom line was that we still were in the midst of a three-game losing streak. When considering that the season before we only lost a grand total of three games throughout the entire regular season, a three-game losing streak seemed pretty inconceivable to me.

At this point in the season, not only was our team having trouble collectively keeping it together, but Evan was also having a hard time getting his head on straight. After starting the season coming off the bench and playing only about a quarter of every game, toward the middle of the season Evan emerged as a legitimate scoring threat and became a starter for the rest of the year. In the Tennessee game, he played all but three minutes and had by far his best game of the year with 21 points, 10 rebounds, and 3 assists. Halfway through his freshman season, it seemed as though Evan had finally gotten the hang of college basketball, with the operative word here being "seemed."

As I alluded to earlier, Evan honestly believed that he would be a clear-cut All-American if his teammates and coaches were not actively working against him to keep him down (which we obviously weren't). For him, the Tennessee game validated what he had thought all along—that not only should he be starting, but he should also be the focal point of our offense. But because the coaches and other players supposedly hated him, he knew this would never happen. Pair this mind-set with the fact that he was one to kick a basketball across the gym during practice if he missed a few shots in a row and it's easy to see how an Evan Turner meltdown was a common occurrence throughout that year.

At a practice shortly after the Tennessee game, Coach Matta became fed up with Evan and gave him an ultimatum. He announced:

"I've scheduled this practice for an hour and a half. That's only 90 minutes. Today we're going to see how long it takes before Evan loses his mind. I've got the countdown on my watch and if Evan lasts the entire 90 minutes without a meltdown, the team won't run today. But if he freaks out, we'll run a suicide for every minute left on the countdown. So, for example, if he loses it an hour into practice, everyone will run 30 suicides. Evan, the entire team's fate lies in your hands. Don't let your teammates down."

I scanned the group of guys in the huddle and noticed that Evan was the only one who looked even slightly confident that we weren't going to have to run, which conveyed to me that he was the only one on the team who wasn't aware that he had the propensity to suddenly turn batshit insane. But the rest of us must have sold Evan short, because the first hour of practice went by without a hitch. When something happened that would've normally led to Evan cursing at the top of his lungs or drop-kicking a ball across the gym, he would calmly collect himself and shrug it off. It was as if we were all watching Bizarro Evan for that first hour of practice. But these little annoyances started adding up, and things turned south real quick. Toward the end of practice he missed a few shots in a row and clenched his fists in anger. Then a pass to a teammate slipped through the teammate's hands and went out of bounds, prompting Evan to quickly turn around, sprint back to the other end of the court for defense, and take a handful of deep breaths in an exaggerated way. It was obvious that Evan was getting dangerously close to blowing a gasket, but luckily, practice ended before the inevitable meltdown came.

Knowing just how big a bullet we had dodged, the guys high-fived each other in celebration and huddled around Coach Matta for his post-practice speech. As Coach started to mockingly congratulate Evan, he looked at his watch and noticed we had finished practice a little early. There were still 10 minutes left on the Melt-down Countdown, so he told us all to spend the last moments of our apparent victory by working on our free throws. When we broke the huddle and headed for the various baskets in our practice gym, Coach Matta stopped me and told me to go to the basket Evan went to.

It didn't take long for me to put the pieces together. After all, Evan and I had a history of flat out disliking one another, and Coach had just explained how the day's practice was going to test Evan's mental strength. It only made sense that I was to be the final test. Sure Evan could withstand missing shots and teammates screwing up, but the only way to really prove that he could keep his composure was to see if he could tolerate me for 10 minutes. In other words, if this practice was Evan's own little game of "Super Mario World," everything that happened in the first 80 minutes could be thought of as just the Koopa Troopas or those bullets with faces on them, and the last 10 minutes with me were like going up against Bowser in that clown helicopter thing. And unfortunately for Evan (and in this case the rest of our team), so long as the game in question isn't any of the Mario Karts, defeating Bowser is never an easy feat.

When I walked over to Evan's basket, he smacked his lips and said, "What are you doing over here, walk-on?" while in the middle of one of his free throws. (Yes, he called me "walk-on.")

I explained that Coach Matta had asked me to shoot with him and that we were supposed to shoot five free throws at a time before we switched. He seemed cool with this, shot his five free throws, and then stepped off the free throw line to switch spots with me without any trouble. And that's when, to put it eloquently, shit went down.

Before I go any further with this story, it should be noted that I faced up to 10 suicides if Evan lost his cool, so it's not as if I was actively trying to piss him off. But as I soon found out, I didn't have to try with Evan. As we switched spots, I handed him the ball and asked him to toss me a bounce pass once I got lined up, just like a referee would do if I were shooting free throws in a game. But he apparently interpreted this as "roll the ball on the ground before I even get set so it hits my feet, makes me bend over, and completely destroys my rhythm." I picked the ball up and got situated at the free throw line before I gently tossed it back to Evan and again asked him to throw me a bounce pass. This time he fired a chest pass at me.

Now, I admit that I probably should've taken the high road at this point and just shot the free throws, but my pride kicked in and wouldn't let Evan get the best of me, so I threw the ball back and once again asked him to simply throw me a bounce pass. As soon as the ball hit his hands, he rocketed it right back and yelled, "Just shoot the fucking ball!" so loudly that he got the attention of everyone in the gym, including Coach Matta. But instead of blowing his whistle and making us run, Coach decided to sit back and watch everything unfold.

I shot my free throws and switched spots with Evan, who had been standing underneath the basket rebounding for me (and throwing passes back to me as hard as he could). As we walked past each other, Evan called me a bitch under his breath and threw his shoulder at my face, connecting square with my chin. Coach Matta instantly blew his whistle and yelled, "There it is! Everyone on the line!"

And with that, Evan had finally had his meltdown.

Once we got situated to start our sprints, Coach Matta said, "Evan, you were so close to making it 90 minutes without losing your mind, but you came up a little short. According to my watch, you made it 87 minutes, which means the whole team has three suicides."

I glanced over at Evan and noticed he was visibly angrier than I've ever seen any human being in my life (he was so mad he had tears welling in his eyes), and even though I was about to run some excruciating sprints, I couldn't help but sport a huge smile across my face.

After the sprints and Coach Matta's second post-practice speech, Evan approached me for what I thought was going to be a conversation to bury the hatchet. But before he said a word, he presented his peace offering in the form of a punch directed at my face. I quickly ducked, gave him a little shove, and walked back down to the locker room, laughing at him. To give you an idea of just how crazy Evan was, consider this: back in the locker room, my teammates scolded *me* for Evan's outburst. That's right—I was being blamed for Evan's inability to keep his cool, because I should've known better and done everything in my power to make sure Evan maintained at least a tiny bit of sanity, since it was obvious he couldn't do it on his own.

Evan and I had had a handful of altercations throughout the year up to that point, but this incident marked the moment that I realized there was a good chance that he and I would never really get along for the rest of our careers as teammates. About a year later, I nicknamed Evan "The Villain" because of constant instances like this and because—let's be honest—it fit him perfectly since he seemed to embrace being the bad guy and being "misunderstood." But while that nickname wouldn't come until later, this altercation definitely marked the moment when he stopped being Evan Turner to me and instead became The Villain.

EIGHTEEN

Despite all evidence to the contrary, The Villain's mental meltdown disguised as a practice somehow actually seemed to help our team, because we went on a three-game win streak and improved our record to 15–6. Of those three wins, the last game at Penn State was undoubtedly the most memorable because—you're never going to believe this—I made another one of my teammates so infuriated on the plane ride back home that I honestly thought he was about to murder me and eat my corpse.

The day before the game, a huge snowstorm was set to hit both Ohio and Pennsylvania, so we pushed our flight out of Columbus up a few hours to avoid any problems getting to Happy Valley. We landed in Pennsylvania without any trouble, but what we weren't prepared for was the follow-up snowstorm on the day of the game that made our return flight a real challenge.

Even though it was customary for us to fly back to Columbus immediately after a game no matter how late it might have been (I once crawled into my apartment bed at 4:00 a.m. after a road game), we initially considered spending the night in Happy Valley. But in the end, the flight control people thought that all we needed was a quick plow of the runway and some de-icer on the plane and we'd be good to go. Since I'm not real fond of telling people how to do their jobs, I figured that if the conditions were good enough for the pilots, they were good enough for me too. (This is the same reason why porn doesn't do it for me. I find it extremely condescending for the girl in porn scenes to repeatedly tell the guy, "Oh yeah, just like that," or, "Give it to me harder," or whatever. The dude is a professional at having sex. I think he knows what he's doing.) Othello Hunter, on the other hand, didn't feel the same way.

After being teammates with Othello for a year and a half, I thought that I had a pretty good idea of just how terrified he was of flying, but apparently I completely underestimated his fear. Following a shaky takeoff, the pilot announced that there was heavy turbulence ahead and we needed to return to our seats and put on our seat belts.

Othello looked concerned and strapped himself into his seat as tightly as he could. The turbulence was initially nothing more than some mild shaking of the plane, but after a couple minutes things got serious and the plane went into a free fall for at least one full second. Now, the only time I like free falling is when I'm singing along with Tom Petty and I've got a few Bud diesels running through my system, so it's not like I was entirely calm in the face of disaster like the *Titanic* band or anything. But the fact of the matter was that I was a huge fan of *Lost*, so I didn't completely panic. That's because even though we were flying over Pennsylvania, I thought there was still a chance we would crash on a strange remote island in the Pacific Ocean, which would've finally given me the chance to murder Jack for being such a douche and a terrible leader, party with Sawyer and Hurley 'cause they're awesome, and try to bang Juliet because her boobs were so godlike I honestly thought that they were Jacob for most of the series. Anyway, my point is that the free fall certainly concerned me and made me wish we weren't 25,000 feet in the air, but I wasn't in a complete state of hysteria like Othello was. And by that I mean that I didn't have an intense scowl on my face, I wasn't pouring sweat, I hadn't inexplicably ripped my shirt off, and I wasn't squeezing the armrests like they were my husband's testicles and I was a housewife who had just caught him cheating with his secretary.

Looking back, the intensity on Othello's face effectively portrayed both how terrified he was and how serious the situation was, which should have made him off-limits for any jokes, but I just couldn't resist and convinced myself that it was just another one of those times when things seemed really serious but we'd all just look back on it and laugh someday. This was mistake number one. Mistake number two was forgetting that Othello wasn't exactly a big fan of mine at the time. That's because after witnessing Matt Terwilliger jokingly call Othello "Simba" or "Mufasa" for a few weeks, due to Othello's African heritage (his parents were both born in Africa), I decided to get in on the action and yell that "Naaaaaaaants ingonyaaaaaaa ma baghiti baba!" intro from the "Circle of Life" song whenever Othello walked into a room. (Sure it was racially insensitive, but it was also funny so that makes it okay.) Apparently Othello was cool with Matt making fun of him (maybe because his real first name was Tegba, so Simba and Mufasa weren't really that far off), but I took it too far with my butchered Zulu. Anyway, in the midst of a terrifying bout of turbulence on a plane back from Penn State, I disregarded both of these warning signs and said:

"Hey, Othello. Just think—if we crash, there's a good chance they'll make a movie about us. We could be the sequel to *We Are Marshall.*"

Yes, I know it wasn't even that funny and was a little offensive, but the point wasn't to make light of a tragedy. The point was to try to get Othello to freak out even more, which I thought would be the funny payoff. But, boy, was I wrong. Othello looked at me to acknowledge the comment, turned his head back toward the front of the plane, and sat in silence for the rest of the flight with the same look of terror on his face that he had already had.

I can't begin to explain how frightened this made me. It's like in high school when you stole your dad's car after he went to bed so you could go to a kegger on the outskirts of town and you got arrested at three in the morning for having an open bottle of SoCo on the dashboard and a bag of weed in the cup-holder. You could've sworn your dad was going to kill you, but instead he just said, "Son, I'm not mad at you. I'm just disappointed in you," and that somehow hurt so much worse. That's kinda how this felt for me. Only now my "dad" was 6'9", 230 pounds, and possessed the anger of a thousand Mel Gibsons.

I kept my head on a swivel the entire rest of the flight (spoiler alert: we landed safely) and genuinely thought Othello was going to try to punch me in the back of the head when I wasn't looking. To make matters worse, I forgot to consider that Othello always sat one seat behind me on our team bus, so the trip from the airport back to campus was one that consisted of me completely turned around in my seat to keep an eye on him. But he didn't say a word. In fact, he didn't speak to me for almost two weeks after the incident, which made things really awkward in the locker room considering he and I had lockers right next to each other.

He ultimately never did anything to get me back, but in a way his lack of retaliation was more effective than anything he could've possibly done because the anticipation haunted me for the rest of the season. And while he's since forgiven me and we're now pretty friendly toward each other, my prediction of "we're all going to look back on this and laugh someday" couldn't be further from the truth. The last time I reminded him of the incident, he almost got as upset as if it were happening again and stressed to me that it wasn't funny then and wasn't funny now. So, if you ever see Othello, do me a favor and refrain from asking him about this story. It's probably best for his sake—and definitely best for my sake—that he not be reminded of it.

In staying true to the roller-coaster season we had been having, we lost on the road in our next game to the same Iowa team that we had beaten by 31 less than a month earlier. Most NCAA Tournament projections had had us solidly in the tournament, but after that loss we found ourselves in the middle of the bubble discussion, which felt foreign considering the season we had had the year before. Nonetheless, we got back on the right track with a win over Michigan, and while it didn't do much to help our chances at making the tournament, losing would've been devastating because Michigan kinda blew. Plus, it was a big game because it was Michigan and it's common knowledge among Ohio State athletes and fans that no opportunity to donkey-punch the Wolverines should ever be taken for granted.

After Michigan gargled our balls, we lost at 13th-ranked Indiana before getting back on track by beating the piss out of Northwestern to set up a rematch with Michigan in Ann Arbor. But thanks to terrible defense in the second half, we blew our opportunity to sweep Michigan and lost by 10. This was doubly bad considering it was the first time Ohio State lost to Michigan in basketball since Coach Matta took over in 2004, and the loss almost certainly put us on the outside looking in as far as the NCAA Tournament was concerned.

With a 17–9 record and only five regular-season games left, it was now officially time to start panicking. Luckily for us, though, the 10th-ranked Wisconsin Buzzcuts were coming into our place, we had a week to prepare, and a win against them would put us right back in the thick of things. But unluckily for us, in the days leading up to that game our team captain and best player cursed out an assistant coach and quit the team in what was undoubtedly my single favorite memory from that season.

NINETEEN

In the brief time we were teammates, the one constant with Jamar Butler was that he was never submissive to authority and pretty much just did whatever he wanted, whenever he wanted. Simply put, I've never met anyone in my life who has either thought to themselves or actually said the phrase "I don't give a shit" more than Jamar. This often made him entertaining, such as when I met him for the first time at a house party on campus during my freshman year and while we were walking from one party to another he whipped his dong out on a crowded sidewalk, pointed it to the side, and took a leak without breaking stride or even making any attempt whatsoever to conceal what he was doing. Another time he got confrontational with our director of basketball operations, Dave Egelhoff, and yelled, "Don't come at me with that bullshit, Dave," during a practice because Dave had apparently come at him with bullshit in the form of a report that Jamar had skipped one of his classes and thus, as a team rule, now had to run disciplinary sprints with our strength coach.

But other times I hated his defiance of authority because it directly affected me in a negative way, such as when, after the National Championship game in 2007, he came into my hotel room, took all the alcohol from our minibar, and consequently racked up a $150 charge on our room that Danny and I had to deal with the next morning. (We didn't have to pay for it, but we still had to convince our coaches that we weren't the ones who were responsible for all the missing liquor, which was surprisingly more difficult than it should've been.) And then there was the practice leading up to the game against the Buzzcuts, when Jamar's defiance reached unprecedented heights.

Before I get to the good part of the story, let me first set the stage. During my time at Ohio State, we typically ended practices with a mini-intrasquad scrimmage that lasted four minutes, since four minutes was theoretically the longest we'd ever have to be on the court at one time during actual games, because the built-in media timeouts occurred at four-minute intervals. Coach Matta was obsessed with getting us to play as hard and as well as we possibly could for four minutes at a time, and he approached every game with the mind-set that we were actually playing 10 four-minute games, or "four-minute wars," as he liked to call them. (It always bugged me that he didn't call them "four-minute battles," since the analogy would work much better if you treated the entire game as a war and each of the 10 segments as battles, but whatever.)

We often ended practice with just one four-minute war, but because we had a week off in between our game with Michigan and our game with the Buzzcuts and therefore didn't need to be too concerned with resting our legs, Coach decided to raise the stakes and end practice with a best-of-three series of four-minute wars, with the losing team having to run a double suicide. After it worked so well and brought our team together so much at the SWAT obstacle course, we split into the same two teams, with the veterans on one team and the new guys on the other.

The first two four-minute wars were boring and are entirely irrelevant to the story, so I'll just tell you that the new guys won the first and we won the second, and we'll move on. In fact, we'll just advance the story all the way to the waning moments of the third and deciding four-minute war, where we found ourselves down by three with 20 seconds left. Now, if you remember the story from earlier about how Daequan snubbed me in an AAU game instead of running the play that was drawn up in the huddle, then you might be getting ahead of yourself here and think that this situation is headed in the same direction.

Instead of checking in after sitting on the bench for the entire game, this time I actually played a ton and, believe it or not, had plays drawn up for me throughout the scrimmages because I was shooting the ball so well. I had been so good, in fact, that I kind of expected the final play to go to me, but our assistant coach made the foolish decision to put the ball in Jamar's hands instead, most likely because he was our leading scorer and senior captain and I was just some pudgy sophomore walk-on. But luckily for our coach, I was able to save his ass and absolve him of the inexcusable sin of breaking the golden rule of basketball, otherwise known as "getting the rock to the man with the hot hand."

The assistant coach's plan was for Jamar to wait until the clock wound down to 10 seconds, come off a ball screen, create separation from the defense, and let a three fly. And that's *almost* what happened. The only problem, though, was that the whole creating separation thing was kinda tricky because the defense knew what was coming, so when Jamar came off of Othello's ball screen, it provided a chance for whoever was guarding Othello to double-team Jamar. With two guys in his face, Jamar was forced to shoot a fadeaway three that never had much of a chance and clanked off the front of the rim (sound familiar?).

But since Othello's defender had left him wide open, Othello had a clear path to the basket and grabbed the rebound with about five seconds left. His instincts kicked in, and he took a forceful dribble to power his way toward the basket for a layup, but we were down by three, so I yelled to get his attention and help him realize that a layup wouldn't have helped us at all. It must've worked because he jumped, changed his mind midair, and threw a pass across the court in my direction. I took a couple of steps to where the ball was headed, caught it, and released the shot just before the buzzer sounded.

Swish.

Duh.

After I hit the scrimmage-tying shot at the buzzer, the gym exploded in pandemonium, and by that I mean I sought out The Villain and executed the "suck it" crotch chop in his face and Othello and a few of my teammates jumped on my back in celebration. It was the biggest shot I ever made in my career at Ohio State, and even though it didn't happen in an actual game, it didn't make it any less significant for me because our practices were always games to me (and our games were always off days). As amazing as it was to save our team from a double suicide, even more impressive was that I managed to get Othello to forget about the plane ride from Penn State for a brief moment, as evidenced by the fact that he gave me an excited bear hug and softly whispered in my ear that he would always be my BFF. (Note: that last part might be revisionist history.) Sadly, this burying of the hatchet was short-lived because of Jamar.

To settle the tie, Coach Matta had us play an overtime period in which the first team to score five points would win. I was hoping we would settle the tie like all normal, civilized human beings settle ties: a group game of "Mercy" with the last man standing claiming the win for his team. But I guess Coach Matta's idea seemed like a fair alternative. Anyway, we won the tip and got the ball, but we couldn't capitalize on our first possession because Jamar got hammered on a drive to the basket and Coach Groce, who was one of our assistant coaches (the same coach who conned me into agreeing to be a manager and is now the head coach at Ohio University), decided to not call a foul. As he ran back on defense, Jamar had some words for Coach Groce (one of which started with "b" and rhymed with "bullshit"), but it was really nothing more than your standard, run-of-the-mill instance of a player cursing out a coach. Standard, that is, until less than a minute later.

Twenty seconds after not getting the foul called for him, Jamar was floored by a blatant moving screen set by Kosta to free up whoever it was Jamar was defending. Again, Coach Groce swallowed his whistle and told Jamar to get up while whoever Jamar was guarding sank a wide-open three. And again Jamar wasn't exactly thrilled with not getting a foul called in his favor. As he got up off the ground, he yelled, "That's fucking bullshit," directly at Coach Groce while slowly dribbling the ball back up the court.

This was the last straw for Groce. He chimed back with "What's that, Jamar?" even though he had obviously heard Jamar the first time.

Jamar walked toward Groce and emphatically repeated himself. "That's fucking bullshit and you know it."

With things rapidly escalating out of control, Groce did the only thing he really could've done in that situation—he called a technical foul on Jamar and threatened to call a second if Jamar didn't calm down.

As I'm sure you could have guessed, neither the first tech nor the threat of a second had any effect whatsoever on Jamar, as evidenced by the fact that he straight up told Groce: "I don't give a fuck about your technicals."

Groce decided to test how true this statement was and rang Jamar up for a second tech, and actually said, "You're outta here!" as he did that hand motion umpires do when they eject guys from baseball games.

Once again, this did nothing to deter Jamar. He told Groce he didn't care if he was ejected because he didn't want to be there anyway, and he started back to the locker room, sprinkling in another handful of nasty curse words. But before he could get off the court, Groce, honest to God, called a third technical foul on Jamar, despite the fact that Jamar had already been "ejected" and had already received the maximum number of techs one player can get in a single game. This third tech triggered yet another outburst from Jamar, which was really nothing more than a bunch of

F-bombs capped off with him telling Groce to "suck my dick" as he finally made his way to the locker room.

Unable to just let it go without getting the last word, Groce—I kid you not—called a fourth tech on Jamar, and in doing so broke the record set by Ted Valentine, who rang up Bob Knight for a then-unprecedented three techs in a game between Indiana and Illinois in 1998. By now, most of the guys on the team and even Coach Matta couldn't hold back the laughter, thanks to the combination of Jamar's anger management issues and Groce's serious commitment to staying in character as a referee instead of embracing his role as assistant coach and attempting to diffuse the problem. But I didn't laugh for long because once the dust settled, the new guys were granted eight free throws as a result of Jamar's four techs and only had to hit two of the eight to clinch the win. They made the first two they shot, my team ran a double suicide, and just like that the biggest shot of my Ohio State career was made entirely irrelevant (since, ya know, it was such a relevant shot before all of that happened).

In all honesty, if the Bananas in Pajamas would have somehow teleported themselves to our arena, walked out to midcourt, started 69ing, and then finished each other off with a couple rusty trombones before sprouting wings and flying away, I still don't think I would have been as genuinely shocked as I was when all this went down. Jamar had a history of being stubborn with authority, but never would I have thought he'd get borderline violent with one of our coaches just because he didn't get a couple fouls called for him. (In his defense, they really were inexcusably bad no-calls.) That in and of itself was pretty crazy, and then Coach Groce took it to another level by not only refusing to break character as a referee (he was like those Pioneer Village people from *South Park* who were a little too committed to acting like it was 1864), but also calling a laughable number of technical fouls as if imaginary techs in an intrasquad scrimmage that was closed to the public were really going to calm Jamar down. (I like to think that before he called each of his last three techs, Groce thought to himself, *This time it* has to *work*.) But most incredible of all, Jamar's tirade erased the greatest on-court accomplishment of my Ohio State career and the one thing I thought was going to help squash Othello's beef with me. And all of this happened in a matter of minutes. I was speechless.

I guess Jamar's outburst was inevitable considering that he announced on a daily basis in the locker room how many days were left until his career at Ohio State was finally over. Plus, after being able to regularly challenge authority without consequence, it was only a matter of time before he tested his limit and everything boiled over. Obviously a lot of the blame lies with Jamar, but it should also be noted that throughout the season our coaches enabled his defiant behavior more than those *Family Feud* contestants who enable their teammates' stupidity by saying "Good answer" when their teammate responds to "Name a U.S. president" with "Chicken nuggets."

He truly did get away with anything he wanted all season, so when he was a no-show for practice the next two days (he eventually came to practice three days after the incident and went about his business as if nothing ever happened and he hadn't literally walked out on his teammates) and was only punished by being forced to sit out the first four minutes of the Wisconsin game, well, let's just say I wasn't too surprised. After all, because we were on the bubble for an NCAA Tournament berth, the game against the Buzzcuts was a must-win for us, and it was clear that we had no shot of winning without Jamar. So we basically sold our souls by giving him a slap on the wrist even though he probably should have been suspended for at least one game if not kicked off the team altogether, and then we looked even worse when we still lost to the Buzzcuts by five.

The truth is that the only reason I complain about Jamar is because I'm jealous. I've always thought he was a good guy underneath his tough exterior, and he certainly was always nice to me when he probably could have justifiably punched me in the throat on a few occasions. Sure we were never best friends, but I did go to his wedding in 2008, and should I get invited, I'll definitely go to his second, third, and even fourth weddings too. Like I said, other than killing my moment of glory in practice, my only issue with him was that I was jealous that he could essentially quit the team for two days after telling one of our coaches to F off and go on and on about how badly he wanted to leave, and only be punished with a four-minute suspension (and, of course, four technical fouls in practice). Meanwhile, when I simply (and respectfully, I might add) called my high school coach an asshole after he asked me for my honest opinion, I had to sit out the entire first half of one of our biggest games of the year and lost my chance at going to Harvard. It just wasn't fair.

Even though we were still considered to be on the bubble after the Wisconsin loss, I was pretty sure that after blowing that game we had virtually no shot at making the NCAA Tournament. We were 17–10 and had four games left in the regular season, with three against ranked teams and two on the road. Sure playing ranked teams and road games provided us with some great opportunities to play our way back into the tournament with some quality wins, but with all of these games coming on the heels of the Jamar debacle, it was pretty obvious to me that there was a better chance of finding an astrophysicist in an AND1 Mixtape Tour audience than there was of us coming together as a team to make one last push for the tournament. But then again, every sports movie ever made revolves around a player or team achieving the impossible, so could it be that all that had happened throughout the year was just the setup for us to circle the wagons and make an unbelievable and dramatic run at the end of the season?

The answer is no. No, it couldn't.

We followed up the Wisconsin loss with a three-point loss at 12th-ranked Indiana that was really only close because Indiana's coach, Kelvin Sampson, had resigned less than a week earlier and Indiana was in just as much disarray as we were. Again, it was an understandable loss considering Indiana was a highly ranked team playing at home, but in order to make the tournament, at some point you need to actually pull out the wins in these games. You also need to make sure that if you're in the midst of a three-game losing streak toward the end of the season (and it's the second three-game losing streak of the year), you don't get blown out by 14 to an unranked Minnesota team in your next game, which is exactly what we did after the IU loss. And even though we eventually somehow closed out the regular season with a couple big wins against 15th-ranked Purdue and 18th-ranked Michigan State, it appeared as if the damage had already been done.

Unfortunately, that suspicion was confirmed in our next game, as a loss to Michigan State in the first round of the Big Ten Tournament prompted Joe Lunardi to tell us to prepare our anus for Selection Sunday because there was no way in hell we were getting a bid to the NCAA Tournament.

TWENTY

If there's one thing I learned during my four years of playing college basketball, it's that—with the exception of his affinity for wearing turtlenecks underneath his blazers—Joe Lunardi never makes a wrong decision in March. Never. The dude predicts who will make the NCAA Tournament every year a lot like Mark May predicts Ohio State football games, with the only real differences being that he substitutes terrible predictions for predictions that always turn out to be right, he doesn't show bias against a team that he's been butt-hurt over for the last 30 years, he actually knows what he's talking about, and he isn't a complete and utter douche. Anyway, the freshmen on our team were unaware of Lunardi's brilliance and foolishly thought he could be wrong in thinking that we wouldn't make the tournament. But I knew better.

We were 19–13 with a 3–9 record against ranked teams, our best player quit the team for two days without any real repercussions, our second-best player (Kosta) was an outcast, and our third-best player (The Villain) was crazy enough to try to start a fight with a walk-on over a bounce pass. According to the Elias Sports Bureau, no team with all of those things on their résumé had ever made the NCAA Tournament in the history of college basketball. And it wasn't in the cards for us to be the first, because when we gathered in the locker room to watch CBS's *NCAA Tournament Selection Show*, Greg Gumbel confirmed the inevitable—we didn't make the NCAA Tournament and would have to settle for the NIT instead.

As a consolation, we were given the number-one overall seed in the NIT, which was basically another way of saying that we had the best mediocre season of any team in the country. For our first game, we drew North Carolina–Asheville, led by Kenny George, who stood seven feet seven inches tall, weighed 370 pounds, and very well may have had a bigger penis than I did. But in the end, his penis did him no good in our game, as we cruised to an 18-point win in which I got to play in the final minute and do a whole lot of nothing. Our win over Asheville sent us to the second round, where we blew out Cal in a game that was played in St. John Arena (the old gym on Ohio State's campus) because I'm pretty sure our arena (Schottenstein Center) was being used for a monster truck rally. The change in venues did nothing to deter my performance, though, as I was able to again stand in the corner and not even touch the ball as I watched the final half-minute of the game tick off the clock.

Our third-round game was back in the Schottenstein Center against Dayton in front of a capacity crowd with a trip to the NIT semifinals at Madison Square Garden in New York City on the line. (You bet your ass I just used nine prepositions in a single sentence.) Because Dayton is just an hour's drive from Columbus, the Flyers brought a ton of fans with them and really fed off that huge block of support as they completely outplayed us in the first half and took a one-point lead into halftime. But in the second half, we came out like our dicks were on fire, took complete control of the game, and ballooned our lead to as many as 18 points before ultimately winning by 11. Other than the fact that it sent us back to the Big Apple for the second time that season, what made this game so memorable for me was that it marked the one and only time during my college career in which I talked trash on the court during an actual game.

I checked in for the game's final minute and fully expected to go through the motions as usual and just run out the clock. But Dayton had other ideas. After making a shot with 53 seconds left to cut our lead to 13, they applied a full-court press and put me in the uncomfortable position of having to actually exert effort on the court, which was a concept that was pretty foreign to me at that point of the season. Dayton's fans and the commentators most likely thought it was inspiring to see the Flyers not give up and keep playing hard until the final buzzer, but my grandmother taught me a couple of different words for it—hogwash and phooey.

I felt like I needed to express my displeasure to the Dayton player who was tightly guarding me 90 feet from the basket despite the game being all but over, and did so by saying, "Listen, guy. I'm a walk-on, we're blowing you out, and there's less than a minute left to play. Face it—this game is over. So in the words of Ludacris, 'Get back, motherfucker. You don't know me like that.' "

I thought I had made an emphatic point, but the Dayton guy wasn't interested and told me to "shut up, bitch."

I said okay, jogged to the other end of the court so my teammates wouldn't pass to me, and in doing so hung them out to dry because my absence in the backcourt made it harder for them to break the press. Sure it may have been selfish, but it also prevented me from having to dribble up the court while under heavy pressure. I regret nothing.

Beating Dayton earned us the right to play Ole Miss in the NIT semifinals in New York City, which is coincidentally where our season essentially started. But unlike our last trip to the Big Apple, we won our first game of the trip by beating Ole Miss without too much trouble, which set up a game against UMass in the championship for all the NIT marbles. In the other semifinal game, UMass had beat Florida, and in doing so they killed the possibility of us playing the Gators in the NIT championship just one year after playing them in the National Championship, which would have been the first time such a thing had ever happened.

UMass used the same up-tempo attack and high-pressure defense against us that they used to beat Florida, and in the first half we had just as much trouble with their frenetic pace as Florida did. We were out-rebounded, out-hustled, and most importantly, outscored, as UMass's lead swelled to double digits with just four minutes left in the first half. We ultimately got the lead down to five at halftime, but even still, we were clearly the better team and should have been having our way with them.

Throughout most of the NIT, our guys seemed disinterested on the court because the NIT was a pointless tournament. And they were able to get away with this because we were so much better than the other teams we played that we didn't have to play 100 percent to beat them. Well, this time around, UMass wasn't exactly a pushover like some of the other teams we played were. So to get through to my teammates and get them to play as well as they should have been playing, I decided to give them a pep talk in the locker room at halftime.

"With the exception of genocide and pedophilia, do you guys know what's worse than playing in the NIT? Losing in the NIT! So get your heads out of your asses, stop feeling sorry for yourselves, and go out there and play like you and I know you're capable of!"

I kind of expected all the guys to jump to their feet, burst into a mosh, tear down our locker room door on their way out to the court, and then proceed to figuratively set UMass on fire and rape all their virgins en route to the NIT Championship. Instead, Coach Matta turned to me and said, "Mark, sit your ass down and don't ever interrupt me while I'm addressing the team again." So yeah, not exactly the reaction I had anticipated.

Even though my speech wasn't well received by Coach Matta, my words apparently came in loud and clear to our players, because we went on a tear in the second half, took the lead within the first two and a half minutes, and never looked back. UMass actually tied the game with about six minutes left, but the game was never in doubt once I saw the fire in our players' eyes right after my pep talk. Thanks to my uplifting words, when the final buzzer ultimately sounded, the scoreboard showed a seven-point advantage in our favor. We were National (Invitation Tournament) Champions.

We spilled onto the court to celebrate, but most of the guys were confused about how excited they were supposed to be. I mean, sure we won the tournament, but at the end of the day it was the NIT and being the best team in the NIT is like being the most attractive Michigan cheerleader or being Canadian. (I really do love you, Canada.) This didn't matter to me, though, because I could see the bigger picture. Beating UMass on that night allowed me to join the likes of George Mikan, Walt "Clyde" Frazier, Ralph Sampson, and Reggie Miller on the list of guys who have won a National (Invitation Tournament) Championship. And that is what's really important—being able to find ways to loosely associate myself with some of the game's greats. No matter where I go or what I do with the rest of my life, I will always share that common bond with these guys, and I will always be a National (Invitation Tournament) Champion. And nobody will ever be able to take that from me.

Well, nobody except the NCAA, who will most likely vacate all four of my years at Ohio State once they find out that I was on all sorts of illicit drugs during my entire career, ranging from anabolic steroids to Adonis DNA. But let's keep that our little secret.

PART FOUR

I don't even know what that is, nor do I care.

—*Coach Matta, when asked for his thoughts on my blog*

TWENTY-ONE

A funny thing happened in between my sophomore and junior seasons at Ohio State, provided that you have a sick sense of humor and think that somebody realizing that their childhood dream is unattainable is a funny thing. Even though everything I've written up to this point would lead you to believe otherwise, the truth is that I actually did take basketball seriously during my first two years in college and I did want to play in the games. But I wanted to play on my terms, which is to say I wanted to play when the game was still in the balance instead of being the human victory cigar that capped off blowout wins.

I screwed around a lot off the court, sure, but during practices I busted my ass and took it just as seriously as everyone else because I wanted to work my way into more playing time. (Okay, I'll admit it was hard for me to write that sentence with a straight face—I really did work hard in practice, but saying I busted my ass and worked as hard as everyone else is probably a slight exaggeration.) Deep down on the inside, I wanted to be a part of the regular rotation of guys and actually play in the first half, but on the outside I masked everything by joking around in the locker room and being way too cool to play hard when I checked in for the final minute of games.

After playing AAU with Greg, Mike, and Daequan for so many years and being regularly called upon to make significant contributions (did I mention that I led the team in scoring a few times? I did? Oh, well this is just another reminder then), I figured that once I walked-on at Ohio State, I would bust my ass and eventually get to play at least a handful of minutes in each game after a few years. My lifelong goal had always been to actually play for a Big Ten basketball team, not to just sit on the bench, so I owed it to myself to give it a legitimate chance. What I failed to consider, though, was that I never actually had any semblance of a chance, no matter how hard or how well I would've played in practice. This was confirmed when Coach Matta admitted to me after I graduated that he would never play a walk-on over a scholarship player under any circumstances ever. (This would've been great information to have when I originally walked-on instead of a month after I was done playing.)

Still, I didn't need to hear him actually admit that he'd never play me because within my first two years it was already obvious that Coach Matta had told my childhood dream and lifelong goal to lick his butthole. In my first two seasons, my status on the team remained entirely unchanged. Actually it got worse, since we had more guys on the team my sophomore season and thus I dropped from 11th man to 12th man on the hypothetical depth chart. And so, when two years of giving it my all and playing the best basketball I had ever and will ever play in my life didn't get me anywhere, I decided to change my focus, just have fun, and stop giving anything that could even remotely be interpreted as a shit.

Close your eyes for a second as you read this and think back to a time when you were in your junior high or high school guidance counselor's office. If the time you are thinking about is when you were bawling your eyes out and whining to your counselor because Jessica Wood called you a loser for having a bunch of Lisa

Frank folders and notebooks, first of all, let me take a second to also laugh at you. Secondly, that's not what I'm talking about, so disregard that thought and instead think about the time that you were talking to your counselor about what you wanted to be when you grew up.

Now think of the time in your life when you realized that what you had always wanted to be was an impossibility. Maybe it was when you figured out that you'd almost certainly never get to be the Emperor of the Holy Roman Empire because it sadly doesn't exist anymore. Or maybe it was when you decided that being a doctor involved way too much school for your liking and/or you weren't smart enough. Or, more likely, you realized that you couldn't be a carnie because you didn't smell like a combination of meth and stale cotton candy, you didn't have a balding mullet, and you weren't missing over half of your teeth. (It's such a shame too, 'cause I would've made an awesome carnie.)

After my sophomore year at Ohio State, I had my realization. No matter how much I had wanted to be a Big Ten basketball star, it was never going to happen. Some would say this made me a failure, but that's an incorrect assessment because before my career was over and my window of opportunity closed, I changed my goal so I wouldn't technically fail. (It's a very popular strategy among us underachievers.) Out was my dream of being a star college basketball player and in its place was my new dream of simply making the most of the cards I was dealt and having as much fun as I possibly could for my last two years of college. In was my dream of embracing everything about my role as a walk-on/benchwarmer for one of college basketball's best programs. In other words, in was the founding of Club Trillion.

TWENTY-TWO

I like to think that the founding of my blog was a lot like the founding of Facebook, or at least how the founding of Facebook was portrayed in *The Social Network*. It wasn't, of course, but I like to think it nonetheless. (I also like to think that my basketball career was a lot like Jesus Shuttlesworth's, my academic career was a lot like Will Hunting's, and my ass-kicking career was a lot like John McClane's—it's more fun that way.) In truth, the only real similarity between the origin of Facebook and the origin of my blog is that they both can be traced back to getting dumped by a girl. I was newly single, living alone in my one-bedroom apartment, and absolutely bored out of my mind because my social skills were terrible and I wasn't much of a partier. One random night in October, I was browsing Facebook (what a coincidence!) and noticed one of my so-called friends posting a bunch of stuff about why everyone should check out his blog.

Since I had nothing better to do, I decided I'd oblige, if for no other reason than he seemed passionate and I felt that I should at least humor him. I clicked on the link he provided and concluded pretty quickly that his blog was awful. The writing was terrible, the topics were uninteresting, and his tone made him sound like a real poopdick. Based on this, you're probably thinking, *Hey, just like your blog! That must be where you got your inspiration!*, and even though you're obviously joking and just trying to be an ass (you don't really mean it, do you?!), you're actually kinda right.

After reading this guy's garbage, I realized that nobody in their right mind would let him write for their site, which meant that he had to have started his blog on his own and had to have been in sole control over everything. It's kind of embarrassing to admit now, but at the time I had no idea what a blog was. Once I read his blog and learned about the concept, though, I figured there was no reason I couldn't do the same thing. And so, since I was bored not only on that night but with life in general, I Googled "create a blog," clicked on the first link provided (which was obviously Google's blogging service, Blogger), and just started writing.

It was entirely my idea to start the blog, but in the beginning it was a three-man operation with Danny and Kyle. Toward the end of the previous season, the three of us formed a bond while sitting on the end of the bench for most of the games. Kyle was a scholarship player and certainly played more than Danny and me, but it wasn't uncommon for him to also sit out entire games and join the two of us in our benchwarmer fun (which primarily just consisted of finding both the most and the least attractive female in the stands). Anyway, the three of us made a concentrated effort to embrace our benchwarming roles and thus decided to reflect our mind-set with the name we gave our group—Club Trillion.

Why Club Trillion, you ask? Well, the "club" part is derived from the fact that there were three of us in the group and we thought of ourselves as a private club, with the only way to gain membership being that you had to be glued to the bench like we were. And the "trillion" part comes from the notion that when we would actually check into the games, we usually played for only one minute and didn't record any statistics—thus our box score showed one minute played followed by 12 zeros, or what we referred to as "a trillion."

(Note: I feel obligated to acknowledge that I didn't come up with the trillion concept. A friend of mine read about it somewhere and told me about it, I loved the idea and shared it with Kyle and Danny, and the three of us decided to fully embrace it. From what I've been told, legendary Philadelphia 76ers statistician Harvey Pollack is credited with coming up with the concept and is therefore kind of the godfather of Club Trillion. Or if I'm the godfather, I guess he could be thought of as the godfather's godfather? I don't know. Point is, I didn't invent the concept, I just made it popular. I just wanted to clear that up.)

Getting a trillion was considered to be a bad thing because it meant you were entirely irrelevant to the game. But we made it a point of pride. Getting a trillion—not recording a single statistic—became our goal whenever we played at the end of games and we actually competed against each other to see who could get the most trillions. Simply put, Club Trillion was out to revolutionize benchwarming, and like Wu-Tang Clan and a broken condom, we wanted to make it crystal clear that we also weren't anything to fuck with.

During the first week of the blog's existence, each member of Club Trillion contributed an introductory post to get the ball rolling, but sometime during the second week Kyle and Danny both decided that blogging about benchwarming was taking things a little too far. After all, Kyle was a scholarship player who had aspirations of actually getting solid playing time (which he eventually did), and writing about how much fun he had on the bench wouldn't exactly send a good message to the fans or, more importantly, the coaches. Danny, on the other hand, had no such aspirations for more playing time. No, he was more concerned with life after playing basketball, as it had always been a lifelong dream of his to get into coaching. He thought that if he was involved with the blog, future potential employers would think he didn't take basketball seriously, which would have been a problem since coaching college basketball kinda requires that he do just that.

And so, they both asked me to delete their posts and eventually to stop acknowledging that they were associated with Club Trillion at all, which I'm sure still haunts them both to this day. Meanwhile, because I had no aspirations for more playing time, no aspirations to coach, and no aspirations to do much of anything, I saw no reason why I should have to stop writing about being a benchwarmer. So Club Trillion marched on, only now it wasn't much of a club since I was the only member.

When Kyle and Danny cut ties with the blog, I was actually kind of happy because it gave me the opportunity to make the blog my own personal thing instead of making it about all three of us. Now I could just write about my experiences at Ohio State (as opposed to our group's collective experiences), and my family and friends back in Indiana could read it to see what I was up to, which was my only real intent with the blog in the first place. Never did I think that anyone outside of my circle of family and friends would care about it, and I certainly had no plan to use the blog as a platform to eventually write a book.

But things changed when I called out the *Columbus Dispatch* in one of my earlier posts for keeping me out of a team picture they were taking for their college basketball preview. They specifically told Danny and me that they didn't want us in the picture (we were the only two guys not in it), so I took to my blog and put them on blast for disrespecting the walk-ons. Again, I was only expecting my family and friends to read it, so I guess you could say it was a bit of a surprise to see Bob Baptist, the OSU basketball beat writer for the *Dispatch*, write about my blog post and playfully defend the *Dispatch* on his own blog. Through his post, all of his followers found out about my blog, came and checked it out, and apparently liked the concept of a benchwarmer giving them inside access to their beloved Buckeyes.

And just like that I had a legitimate audience and suddenly had to shift the focus of everything. No longer was I catering to just my family and friends. Now I had to write less about me specifically and more about both the role of a walk-on for a big-time college basketball team and what some of my superstar teammates were like off the court. Specifically, I had to write about my less than amicable relationship with Evan "The Villain" Turner.

Not long after that initial wave of people found out about my blog from Baptist, I wrote on my blog about how ridiculous it was that The Villain had suddenly started referring to himself as "The Kid" around the locker room and somehow managed to get most of my teammates to call him that within a week or two also. Maybe he and I were raised differently, but where I come from, people have to earn their nicknames and trying to give yourself a nickname just because it sounds cool is not only pathetic but it's borderline offensive. So when he somehow successfully nicknamed himself The Kid, I decided to show him just how immoral his actions were.

I figured the best way to accomplish this was to try to give myself a nickname too, so that way when The Villain noticed how lame and pathetic I was, he would realize that that was exactly the same way he was being perceived. I went with "The Shark," solely because it rhymes with "Mark" and because everyone named Mark has been called "Mark the Shark" at least once in his life. The way I saw it, The Shark was the most uncreative nickname possible and would surely be perfect in showing how stupid self-assigned nicknames are.

Over the course of the next few weeks, I referred to myself as The Shark in the locker room, on my blog, and in public. But instead of showing The Villain how stupid he looked, nicknaming myself had the exact opposite effect. Everyone who followed my blog started calling me "Mark the Shark," or just "Shark." This in turn made me start liking the nickname, and before long my plan had completely backfired. I had not only managed to make every-one call me The Shark, but I had also managed to convince myself that giving myself a nickname wasn't such a bad idea after all. In other words, I had become exactly what I hated.

Since I felt like The Villain had somehow gotten the better

of me after my plan didn't exactly work out how I had hoped, I decided that I should at least give him a new nickname, since "The Kid" made no sense whatsoever. My nickname rhymed with my real name and was kind of badass. His nickname, on the other hand, had no story behind it and no relevant meaning whatsoever, so I decided to do something about it. I came up with "The Villain," not only because he was very much a villain in my own personal life, but also because he had a chip on his shoulder and seemed to embrace being the bad guy as some sort of motivational tactic. Also, since my blog celebrated riding the bench, and since The Villain was morphing into one of the best players in college basketball, the nickname made sense from the standpoint that if walk-ons were going to be thought of as heroes, then superstar players like The Villain had to be the villains.

Now that both of us had pretty sweet nicknames and a bit of mutual disdain for one another, I made our tumultuous relationship the focal point of my blog. In reality, our relationship wasn't nearly as bad as I portrayed it, but we did have real animosity toward one another, so I took it and ran with it.

The people who followed my blog seemed to eat it up, and before long I had ceased being an obscure and unknown walk-on named Mark Titus and had undergone a complete identity change that turned me into The Shark. I welcomed this change with open arms because after being an anonymous walk-on buried on the end of the bench for two years, it was nice to finally get a little respect and attention. Little did I know, though, that this initial attention was nothing compared to the storm that would hit me less than two months later in the form of ESPN's Bill Simmons and his audience of millions. But we'll save that for later.

TWENTY-THREE

As my blog became more and more popular, the concept of the trillion did too. Benchwarmers at all levels around the country emailed me (and still do), either to tell me they planned on getting trillions for their teams or to brag about trillions they had already racked up. Not only were the players on board, but basketball fans in general also loved the idea of the trillion and would rummage through box score after box score to notify me of the guys in NBA and college who were the best at being entirely irrelevant on the basketball court.

With all of this popularity for the trillion came differing interpretations of what exactly a trillion is. After all, some box scores only include points, rebounds, assists, and fouls to go along with minutes played. In these cases, would a steal, blocked shot, turnover, or missed shot ruin the trillion? And what about the guys who play less than a minute and their box score actually reads zero minutes played? Since their box score would just have a bunch of zeroes, they'd technically be putting up a "zero" instead of a "trillion," right?

Well, since I'm kind of the designated authority on all things trillion, I figured that I'd take it upon myself to settle these disputes once and for all. That way, when discrepancies arise in the future, you can just refer to this book for a judgment instead of having to organize a cockfight or a round of jousting to determine a winner like you probably do now. (By the way, that last sentence was a test. If you read "cockfight" and "jousting" and didn't think of chickens and either guys riding horses or the American Gladiators, there's a good chance you're gay—not that there's anything wrong with that.)

With all of that being said, here is my one rule and my three points of emphasis concerning the trillion:

THE RULE: OTHER THAN "MINUTES PLAYED,"
NO STATS WHATSOEVER

This is the one and only rule that applies to getting the trillion, yet somehow so many people can't quite figure it out. It's simple—if you do anything that would be recorded in any basketball scorebook as a statistic, you've ruined your trillion. This means points, rebounds, assists, shots, blocked shots, fouls, technical fouls, steals, turnovers, and anything else I forgot about. The idea of the trillion is that while you played in the game, you might as well have stayed on the bench because you essentially did nothing while you were on the court (good or bad). It celebrates irrelevance, and once you do anything that could be recorded as a statistic, you've had an effect on the game and therefore are no longer irrelevant.

In other words, if a basketball game could be thought of as a movie, then the statistics each player puts up are like lines for each character. In that regard, recording even one statistic is significant because it could take you from being an extra who never has any dialogue (coincidentally, these actors are also referred to as walk-ons) to Rob Schneider making his "You can do it!" cameos in all those Adam Sandler movies. So basically, recording a single statistic makes you the guy responsible for atrocious movies like

The Animal and *The Hot Chick* (although, to be fair, he was the focal point of what was quite possibly my favorite *South Park* bit ever and was pretty solid in *Home Alone 2*). Now try telling me that a foul or steal isn't really that big of a deal.

As far as the "Is playing less than a minute and getting a '0+' in the 'minutes played' column still a trillion?" debate goes, this is also pretty simple—if your ass is on the court when even a single second ticks off the clock, you are eligible for the trillion. You could play the entire 40 minutes of the game or just play for a few seconds. Doesn't matter. As long as your box score doesn't have a DNP (which stands for "did not play"), you have the opportunity to register a trillion.

The thing to keep in mind is that "trillion" shouldn't be taken literally, and by that I mean that you don't have to play exactly one minute and have exactly 12 zeroes in your box score. No, getting a trillion just means you officially played in the game, but you didn't do anything while you were out there. It doesn't matter how much you played. It just matters how much—or more accurately, how little—you did with your time on the court. If you played 40 minutes and didn't do anything, you've just recorded a 40 trillion. And if you played three seconds and didn't do anything, you've just recorded a 0+ trillion. Both are considered trillions, and both are really difficult to pull off for different reasons. (The 40 is tough because the more you play, the greater your chances of recording at least one statistic, and the 0+ is tough because coaches rarely play guys for less than a minute.)

The best possible trillion you can get is a 4 trillion
(play four minutes, no stats)

I've written about this in my blog before, but my guess is that most of you who are reading this are just as familiar with what I've written in my blog as your grandma is with the *2 Girls 1 Cup* video, so I'll explain it again. (By the way, if you weren't thinking about your grandma watching *2 Girls 1 Cup* as you read that, you are now. You're welcome.) Basically the reason the 4 trillion is the most desirable is because anything less isn't as difficult to achieve and anything more means you're a non-benchwarmer who sucks.

In an earlier chapter, I mentioned the concept of a "four-minute war," which is derived from the fact that college basketball games are split into four-minute segments for media purposes. Well, because of these media time-outs in four-minute intervals, it's customary for coaches to wait until after the final media time-out to sub in their scrubs. My theory is that they wait until after the final time-out because it guarantees that they won't have to talk to the scrubs in the huddle and consequently treat them like regular players, which is something coaches clearly want no part of.

Since walk-ons typically only play when there are less than four minutes left, anyone who plays more than four minutes, by implication, is a good enough player to contribute to the team. But if that player records a trillion, he's obviously not contributing anything and is instead just wasting everyone's time. Simply put, the trillion is supposed to celebrate irrelevance, but getting a 5 trillion or higher doesn't make you irrelevant because if you've played five minutes and contributed nothing, you have negatively impacted your team. So you're worse than irrelevant. Big difference.

The ultimate goal is a perfect game

Much as a baseball pitcher can take his no-hitter to another level by not letting anyone on base at all, basketball players can also take their trillions to another level by getting a perfect game of their own. A couple of years ago, I defined a perfect game as a game in which a player not only records a trillion, but does it without even touching the ball. And if you think about it, this really is the epitome of irrelevance, since it means that the player literally did nothing more than run up and down the court a few times and most likely just did his best to stay out of the way. But I've given it some more thought since then and have decided that there needs to be one more stipulation added to the perfect game—a plus-minus of 0.

For those who don't know, a player's "plus-minus" is a relatively new fad of a basketball statistic that tracks his team's success
while he is on the court. So, for example, if you have a plus-minus
of +4, then your team scored four more points than your opponent
in the time you were on the court.

If you play for a minute or two, record no statistics, don't even
touch the ball, *and* have a plus-minus of 0, who is to say you even
played at all? Your time on the court could be completely stricken
from any sort of record of the game and it wouldn't change a single
thing. Without a plus-minus of 0, there's a chance that maybe you
did something to affect the margin of victory (such as set a screen
to free up a teammate, who then hit a shot). But with a plus-minus
of 0, even if you did do something to affect the final score, everything eventually balanced itself out because you gave up just as
many points as you helped score.

If irrelevance is the goal—and we've clearly established that
it is—then there is absolutely no way to play in the game and be
more irrelevant than to record no stats, never touch the ball, and
have a plus-minus of 0. There just isn't. And that's why this new
definition of the perfect game should be the crowning achievement
that all walk-ons strive for. It truly is irrelevance personified.

Blatantly avoiding stats is simply not cool

This is my last point of emphasis but the most important one
because it focuses on maintaining the integrity of the game. Obviously, getting a trillion is easy to do if you put zero effort toward
actually playing basketball the way it was intended to be played,
but that defeats the purpose and strips away the sense of accomplishment. Personally, I'm of the opinion that the only way to really
feel good about your trillion is to play as if the game is tied and
there's only a minute left. I have always been a firm believer in
blocking out on defense, crashing the boards on offense, and even
diving on the floor from time to time if necessary. (All right, so I
might be lying with that last one, but whatever.) Sure this belief put

me in a lot of unfavorable situations, but it also gave me the peace of mind that comes with knowing that I was playing the game the right way.

The fact of the matter is that not everyone who tries to get trillions does so in an honorable manner. Some people give minimal effort to the actual basketball game and instead focus on going out of their way to avoid recording statistics and preserve their trillion. I've heard of guys purposely dodging rebounds that bounce their way, turning down wide-open layups, and even immediately calling time-out to avoid a potential turnover after they picked up their dribble. While I think it's awesome that the trillion has become so popular that some people value it over scoring points or grabbing rebounds, it's unfortunate that they cheapen the trillion by not playing hard.

I don't necessarily expect players to go balls to the wall, but a general rule of thumb is to play hard enough that the coaches and fans can't tell you have an ulterior motive. If someone watching can tell that something is a little off (you run away from rebounds, don't shoot wide-open shots, etc.), you should be ashamed of yourself for not giving the trillion the respect it deserves. But again, this isn't a rule and is merely a suggestion. At the end of the day, it's possible to get a trillion without playing hard. But as far as I'm concerned there's a special place in hell for people who routinely do this. The way I see it, it's kind of like using Oddjob when playing "GoldenEye" on N64—it's not technically against the rules, but there's no denying that you're morally cheating and you're kind of a dick for taking the easy way out.

PART FIVE

I do not think I like you very much.

—*Zisis Sarikopoulos, my teammate from 2008 to 2010,*
10 minutes after we first met

TWENTY-FOUR

By the time the first practice of the 2008–2009 season rolled around, I could already tell that our team that year would be the most ragtag group of misfits I would ever play with. Sure the year before we lacked any sort of leadership whatsoever, underachieved all season, and missed out on the NCAA Tournament, but that wasn't because we were "misfits" per se. No, that was more because our locker room was split right down the middle, with one group consisting of a bunch of jaded assholes with no patience and the other group consisting of know-it-all freshmen who refused to listen.

But the 2008–2009 team was different. I had no doubt in my mind that we would have some measure of success because we actually got along. (Relatively speaking anyway. The only times we didn't were when a couple of guys wanted to fight me, which is something that I probably shouldn't be as proud about as I am.) No, I don't say that we were misfits because we struggled to develop into a cohesive unit. I say we were misfits because our team consisted of what could only be described as "a bunch of characters."

The most prominent of these characters was The Villain, who I'm not sure can even be adequately described with just words. But words are all I've got right now, so I'll give it a try anyway: The Villain was an insecure, socially feebleminded, possibly bipolar, and often callous perfectionist who had all the talent in the world, who lacked self-confidence and the ability to trust in anybody around him, who was actually one of the nicest guys you'll ever meet when he wanted to be, and who would frequently walk around our locker room with his dick flopped over the waistband of his pants. That really is the best description I can possibly give. It should be noted that in his sophomore season he wasn't quite as big of a hothead as he was the season before, but he still consistently made things entertaining.

The incoming freshman class that season, which consisted of BJ Mullens, Will Buford, Anthony "Noopy" Crater, and Walter Offutt, were characters in their own right and were my favorite group of freshmen in my four years at OSU (this includes my own freshman class). Walter was like everyone's little brother and wanted to fit in so badly that he was an easy target to pick on. But it was always just in good fun, as everyone fully respected him and knew that he'd do anything for any one of us. Noopy was exactly like you think a guy named "Noopy" would be and ended up transferring halfway through the season after he tried to fight me in our locker room one day (more on this later). BJ, who now plays for the Oklahoma City Thunder, was the best player of the class and was essentially just a 12-year-old trapped inside an 18-year-old's body, as evidenced by the fact that he thought it was just as funny as everyone else did that his name was "BJ" and he would occasionally make fart noises with his mouth during film sessions just because he could. And like BJ, Will was a McDonald's All-American who was a completely different person on the inside than he appeared to be on the outside.

At first glance, Will might come across as a thug/gangster/ whatever-other-words-white-people-use-to-describe-black-people-they-don't-trust, which is something I'm sure he loves because he prides himself on being from the mean streets of Toledo. But in reality, he's a smart guy who has his head on straight and is as much of a gangster or thug as Kirk Herbstreit's frosted tips. Truth be told, Will is my favorite teammate in any sport at any level for a variety of reasons, with the biggest reason being that he is the only black guy I've ever met in my life who gave me permission to use the N-word whenever I wanted.

Note: As a token of my appreciation for you making it this far in the book, I've decided to take you back to your childhood and make this next part of the book a "choose your own adventure." Only instead of a "choose your own adventure," it's going to be more of a "let the author randomly choose your adventure for you." So, with that being said, I just rolled some dice, flipped a few coins, and ran a crazy and complicated algorithm, and the 100-percent-completely-random-and-therefore-in-no-way-should-be-interpreted-as-racist results that came back said that black people should skip over everything until they get to the bold text at the end of the chapter, and everyone else should start reading the next paragraph like they normally would, but stop reading once they get to the bold text. From there, we'll all meet up as a big group again after the bold text ends and the normal text starts again. Ready, go.

Since it's common knowledge that the one thing all nonblack people have in common is that "get permission from a black guy to drop the N-bomb in his presence" is at or near the top of every one of our bucket lists, I'm guessing you all are dying to know how I was lucky enough to win this coveted golden ticket. Well, believe it or not, it all started when I accidentally let it slip and had no idea what had happened until it was too late. (Funny story: that's also how I lost my virginity.)

I was a bit of an anomaly at Ohio State in that I was one of the few college basketball players in history who preferred country to rap music. And by "country" I mean the countriest of country (George Strait, Tracy Lawrence, Alan Jackson, etc.), not that pop-country stuff that's popular today (like Taylor Swift, Kenny Chesney, Rascal Flatts, etc.). In other words, I don't think my taste in music could've been any more opposite than the rest of my teammates.

Because I was always outnumbered and therefore always had to listen to rap music in the locker room and weight room, I eventually decided to fight back. I burned a handful of country CDs, wrote "Weezy" on all of them (I did some research and learned that Weezy is the nickname of Lil' Wayne, who was the rapper of choice for most of the guys), and then scattered them around the stereo in the weight room in hopes that someone would mistakenly play one. (Our strength coach wouldn't let guys change the music once it started because he wanted us focusing on lifting weights instead of the music.) Every now and then it would work, and everyone would be pissed at me because they'd have to listen to Alabama explain the importance of having a fiddle in the band when playing in Texas instead of listening to the Big Tymers explain the importance of "slapping that bitch" and "punching that ho" when trying to get your roll on. My quest to get country music played in our locker room and weight room was an ongoing battle, and the rare occasions when I succeeded were some of the most rewarding moments in my basketball career.

So what does this music battle have to do with Will letting me drop the N-bomb? Well, I failed to mention that Tupac is my one exception to my disdain for rap music, as he just might be my favorite artist from any genre of all time (strange, I know). But my teammates didn't know this. As far as they could tell, I hated everything about rap music. I successfully kept my love for Tupac under wraps for quite some time, until one day I finally decided to come out of my Tupac closet when Will played "Changes" on the locker room speakers when he and I were the only two guys in the locker room.

It's comforting to know that even at a young age I was a fan of old Converse shoes, long socks, short shorts, America, the Lloyd Christmas haircut, and posing for pictures at Sears.

Even though this was the most hard-fought championship I ever won in my life (we had to win five games in one day to win the thing), I'm pretty sure the only reason I'm smiling is because my dad had just promised to take me to "All You Can Eat Pancakes" at IHOP.

My first year with my new AAU team. As you can tell from the picture, I had no problems fitting in and we were all a fun group of people to be around.

Greg Oden and me after winning the AAU National Championship when we were freshmen in high school.

Greg, Mike Conley, and me in our sophomore year of high school. I know what you're thinking and yes, I did purposely put myself in perfect position to be cropped out of the picture, simply because I was typically cropped out of every picture taken of us three so I figured I'd be courteous and make the inevitable cropping easier.

As you look at Greg's tight-fitting backward hat, big glasses, and calf-high socks with sandals, keep in mind that this picture was taken after we went to a matinee magic show instead of an Ashanti concert. So yeah, I defy you to show me a whiter black guy than 2005 Greg Oden.

Pictured: The envy of the 2006 Brownsburg High School prom.

A group of Wisconsin fans in the Buzzcuts' student section showing their support for Club Trillion.

Left to right: me, Jon Diebler, The Villain (Evan Turner), and David Lighty. I signed the national anthem on the field before kickoff for this Ohio State football game. And no, I didn't mean to say "sang." I signed, as in I performed the lyrics in sign language (which explains the shirt I'm wearing). I'm still not sure why I did this.

Signing autographs on inflatable sharks after my senior night game. It's adorable how that girl on the right doesn't realize that I'm most likely going to be entirely irrelevant in a few years.

Posing for a picture with the "Scarlet Man Group" as the Big Ten Network films a documentary of my senior night. Even though these three guys were some of my favorites in our student section, I don't think "I just scarlet myself" has quite the same ring to it.

Mark Titus Will you Marry Me?

"Just double checking, but this sign is supposed to be a joke and you're not gonna like, stalk me and eventually murder me or anything, right?"

Getting introduced with my family before the game on my senior night. My favorite part of this picture is my dad's look of disgust upon realizing that his crying son is an enormous vagina.

Cutting down the net after winning the 2010 Big Ten championship.

In the locker room after winning the 2007 Big Ten championship my freshman year.

If I had to sum up my four years as a member of the Ohio State basketball team with one picture, this would be it.

At the Ohio State tradition of jumping in Mirror Lake the Thursday night before the OSU–Michigan football game. I like to think that Greg is in the process of telling me I shouldn't expose myself like I am because people could take pictures of me and put them on the internet.

I'm like every other white guy in America: "Changes" is my favorite Tupac song and I've known all the words since I was 14. So when I heard the first couple notes, I thought it would be funny to surprise Will. I called out his name and walked his way. As I approached him, I furrowed my brow, squinted my eyes to look tough, and then rapped the first verse in as close to Tupac's voice as I could get.

I completely caught him off guard, and judging from the fact that he was cracking up, he loved every second of it. But things quickly changed when I got to one particular line:

"Cops give a damn about a Negro. Pull the trigga, kill a nigga, he's a hero."

As soon as I said "nigga" (without the "-er," mind you—I'm told that that's an important detail that shouldn't be overlooked), Will got up in my face and yelled, "What did you just say?!"

Since I had known that song for so long and had sung it in my car by myself countless times, I was essentially on cruise control and honest to God didn't even think about the fact that the song had the word "nigga" in it and I was singing to a black guy. Whoops.

I didn't know Will all that well, so I was convinced he was going to end my life, which explains the terrified look on my face as I stammered, "I . . . I . . . I didn't say anything."

He wasn't satisfied with this. "Yes, you did. Now tell me what it was you just said, honky."

He started smiling, and I realized that he was just screwing with me. But I still didn't know how to respond, so I said, "I was just singing a song. If you think about it, I was quoting Tupac, so you can't even get mad really."

He seemed to agree with this sentiment. "I'm just messing with you. I'm not really mad. But I will be if you don't say 'nigga' again."

This baffled me. "Wait, you actually want me to say it again?"

He said, "Hell, yeah. I've never really heard a white guy say it before. So say it again, cracker."

I couldn't help but laugh as I thought about how much the situation felt kinda like that Chevy Chase and Richard Pryor word association sketch from *Saturday Night Live* in the '70s. I told Will, "I'm not saying it again. I know what you're trying to do, but it's not happening."

He got serious and said, "For real. I won't do anything to you. I just want to hear a white boy say it. I think it's funny. Just say it real quick."

I sensed that he was telling the truth and really did just want to hear a white guy say it. I scanned the locker room to make sure none of my other teammates were in there and then softly said, "Nig-uh. [I made it a point to go over the top with my exaggeration of the 'uh' on the end.] There. You happy?"

Will lost it. As he was wiping the tears from his eyes from laughing so hard, he said, "Man, that was the funniest thing I've ever heard. I can't even get mad at that, it's so funny. You gotta say that again when the rest of the guys are here." I told him that I would never do such a thing, but he insisted. "Listen. I'm telling you that I won't get mad if you say 'nigga.' I won't ever do anything to you. That shit is just too funny to get mad. You gotta say it again tomorrow."

I looked at him in disbelief and realized that he was dead serious. A black man was insisting that I say "nigga" in front of a group of other large black men. I was obviously thrilled about this unprecedented free pass, but I was also equal parts confused and paranoid that it was a trap. It was like picking up a girl for a first date in high school and as we're leaving her dad hands me a couple of condoms, winks at me, and tells me to have fun. *It can't be this simple. There has to be another reason why this is happening.* I left the locker room thoroughly confused.

The next day Will announced what happened the day before to the entire team in the locker room. This piqued the interest of a few of the black guys on the team, who joined Will in trying to persuade me to repeat the offending word, either because they also thought it was funny or because it would've given them an excuse to kick my ass. But despite their best efforts, I adamantly denied that I ever said anything in the first place and never gave in to their request. (I decided that this was probably the best approach.) I kept my mouth shut, got ready for practice, and exhaled a sigh of relief as I walked out of the locker room unscathed.

This saga was far from over, though. Throughout practice, Will continued to harass me by constantly telling me to "just say it real quick" whenever we were standing next to each other on the sidelines, in the middle of drills, and even during the scrimmage at the end of practice. But I stood firm and acted like I didn't know what he was talking about. By the time practice ended, I had denied his request no less than 15 times. It was obvious that he wouldn't be satisfied until I finally gave in.

After practice, I was taking my shoes off in the locker room and saw Will head straight for our refrigerator to grab a Gatorade. I asked Will to get me one since we had lockers close to each other and he was going to walk my way anyway. He obliged and when he handed me my Gatorade, something came over me and told me it was time to make my move and end Will's harassment once and for all. Using my best stereotypical black accent (blackcent?), I casually said, "Thanks, homey, I appreciate it. That's why you my nigga."

Will started walking away for a half-second before suddenly realizing what had happened. Once it hit him, he yelled, "Aw hell naw!" and scanned the room to see if anyone else had heard it. But I was too sly. While Will momentarily lost his mind and tried to get everyone's attention, I calmly walked to the shower and pretended I had no idea what he was talking about. It very well might have been the most smoothly executed moment of my life.

Following this second incident, I realized that Will's permission came with a catch—I was only allowed to drop the N-bomb in my normal, nasally, white guy voice because he thought it sounded funny that way. His reaction made it clear to me that he was desperate for everyone else on the team to hear me say it, so I made it my mission to drive Will crazy for the rest of my career at Ohio

State. Since he insisted on making me uncomfortable, I fought back by saying it when he would be the only one to hear it. Also, since so much of the appeal for him was the fact that I apparently sounded like the world's biggest geek when I said it, I almost always said it in my most stereotypical black accent from then on.

There was, unfortunately, some collateral damage along the way, as a few of the other black guys on the team overheard me a time or two (most of them never got too upset because they knew I was just trying to mess with Will), but for the most part my plan worked perfectly. In fact, sometimes it worked so perfectly that Will had no idea I'd said it at all. I'd subtly throw it in somewhere as I said good-bye to him, I'd nonchalantly sing it whenever we listened to Tupac together, and I'd even sometimes mock him to his face by smacking my lips and saying, "Shhhiiiiiiiiit, nigga," for no reason in particular, just like he always seemed to do. And believe it or not, he often wouldn't even notice. But even when he did notice, he would usually just try to hold back his laughter and pretend to be mad.

Yes, Will Buford was most certainly my favorite teammate I've ever had, and even though to an outsider it might seem like we were playing some sort of offensive and racially insensitive game, the truth is that . . . well . . . I guess we were playing an offensive and racially insensitive game. But it's okay if I was being racist, because Will returned the favor by frequently making fun of white people to me. And everyone knows that combating racism with even more racism always works, so it's totally fine.

Here's the thing you have to understand about white guys: with the exception of getting random erections in public and trying to dance, there is nothing on earth that is consistently more awkward for us than the N-word. Despite what you might think, the truth is that a large majority of us don't have an ounce of racism in our bodies, which is exactly why the N-word is so awk-

ward for us. (If we were racist, we'd just freely use it without regard for anything or anyone.) Some of the best songs, movies, stand-up comedy bits, and just stories in general use the N-word frequently, and while in a perfect world we would love to quote these things to all of our friends, we're absolutely terrified of being overheard and misunderstood by a black guy.

Hell, even when we aren't the ones actually saying the N-word, it's still terrifying for us. Think about it. Have you ever seen/heard a white guy listening to rap music while driving a car? Of course you haven't, because when we see you pull up next to us, we always quickly turn down our stereo to avoid offending you. Obviously this makes no sense because all we're doing is listening to music, but the "rules" surrounding the N-word are so confusing for us that they make us do these nonsensical things. So for a black guy to explicitly tell us that it's okay to say the N-word and we don't have to be worried about being hated or perceived as racist, it's a huge relief because it means that a major source of awkwardness and discomfort for us no longer exists.

But with all of that being said, I declined Will's permission for me to use the N-word whenever I wanted. You see, even though most white guys would've taken this open invitation and abused it in the form of playing some sick and twisted game where they see if they can use the N-word in Will's presence without him realizing it, I'm not like most white guys. I know about the history of the word and the powerful hate behind it that still exists today, and I know that there are a lot of black people who are offended by the word even when other black people are the ones who are using it. I know that racism has been a serious problem in this country since its foundation, and even though things seem to be getting progressively better, we're still a long way from the racially tolerant society that we should have had centuries ago.

The way I saw it, there was just simply nothing good that

could've come from me using this word. Besides, it's not like Will is the representative for all black people in the world. Just because he gave me permission doesn't mean that the other black guys on the team would've been okay with me casually tossing around the most racist and most offensive word in the history of the English language. So when Will said, "Mark, I've been giving it a lot of thought and would like to grant you the rare honor of being able to say the N-word in my presence whenever you want," I had no choice but to respond, "Sorry, Will, but this country has come much too far with our progression of racial tolerance since the end of the Civil War, and especially in the last 20-plus years, for me to just throw that all away now. I would be doing black people a disservice, I would be doing white people a disservice, and most of all, I would be doing the United States of America a disservice if I selfishly accepted your offer. So, I'm sorry, but I have no choice but to decline."

Like the gentleman he is, Will graciously told me he understood my decision. The maturity and respectfulness displayed in that conversation is just one of the many reasons why I think our relationship should be studied by sociologists and used as the consummate example of what true racial tolerance would look like in a utopian society.

So there you have it. As you can see from just this one example, the 2008–2009 team was certainly full of characters. To go along with Evan and the always entertaining freshman class, I had started my blog in the off-season and taken my "not giving a crap" campaign public, so I felt obligated to amplify my antics in practices and during the games so it would make for more interesting posts. When you also consider that two more vibrant personalities returned from the previous season in the form of Dave Lighty (who consistently had more energy than the rest of the guys on the team combined) and Dallas Lauderdale (who would randomly break into song and dance at any time), it's easy to see that while it may have been difficult to determine just how successful we would be on the court, one thing was clear—the 2008–2009 season was certainly not going to be a dull one.

TWENTY-FIVE

We opened up the season with a blowout win against Delaware State, which was a game that would've been pretty boring if not for the fact that it opened my eyes to just how popular my blog was starting to become. When I checked into the game for the final minute, the OSU student section not only started chanting "trill-ion" over and over as a way of encouraging me to do nothing on the court, but they actually rained boos throughout the arena when I pulled down a rebound just a few seconds later and ruined my trillion. (It was the most heavily booed "rebound" since the 2005 Martin Lawrence movie.)

As cool as it was to see our student section getting behind the Club Trillion movement, it was that much weirder to get heckled for something that I had always been applauded for. It was a lot like that fateful day in junior high when you realized that, after being the envy of all your classmates for years, you were suddenly the biggest loser in school for bragging about having a Charizard card. Everything I had learned about the game of basketball was no longer useful, because the trillion had become more than just a cute observation about my irrelevance—it was now my expected way of life.

After squeaking out a four-point win over Bowling Green in our second game of the year, we annihilated what appeared to be Samford's women's team in one of the strangest games I've ever seen. The reason I say it was a strange game (and the reason I say we played their women's team) is because we held Samford to just 22 points, including just six points in the first half, as we cruised to a 59–22 win. To put Samford's dismal offensive display into perspective, consider this: even though I was in street clothes for the game because the day before I hurt my back lifting weights (or more accurately, trying and failing to lift weights), I still scored the same amount of points as three of Samford's starters combined. Furthermore, when you combine my points with The Villain's 16 points, the two of us alone damn near outscored their entire team. And when you combine all of my points, The Villain's 16 points, and the points scored by my other teammates, we outscored their entire team by 37. So yeah, they kinda sucked.

The Samford win set up our first big game of the year at 22nd-ranked Miami, which was a road trip I was really looking forward to thanks to my perception of Miami as a city full of topless babes, Cuban cigars, and pet detectives who talk out of their butthole. Unfortunately, we stayed in Miami for less than 24 hours (and focused most of those hours toward the game) and had no time whatsoever to hit up South Beach, party with hookers on the Miami football yacht, or even find Nevin Shapiro and convince him to pay for abortions for all of our girlfriends. Not all was lost, though. We left Miami with a five-point win, so at least we had something to show for turning down the chance to get wet and wild with all that Miami poon.

We followed that up with two more huge wins, first against seventh-ranked Notre Dame in Indianapolis and then against Butler at home. This string of impressive wins was enough to catapult us to a number-16 ranking, but that wouldn't last long because we destroyed Jacksonville and Iona the following week to jump up to number 13 in the polls. A win against UNC-Asheville in our next game improved our record to 9–0, which was the best start of any of my four seasons at Ohio State, and set up our last big nonconference game of the season, against West Virginia at home.

West Virginia came into the game unranked, but through intensive scouting we knew that they were among the best in the country at playing team defense, playing unselfishly, drinking moonshine, and kissing their sisters. Compounding the fact that they were a formidable and underrated opponent was the fact that Dave Lighty, our captain and the heart and soul of our team, broke his foot against UNC-Asheville and was out for not only the West Virginia game but also for the rest of the season.

Undaunted, we made the college basketball experts eat their words after they didn't give us much of a chance. We battled all night like our backs were against a wall and gritted out what was probably the toughest win of the season for us. And by that I mean that West Virginia fisted our anus so badly that even the goatse guy couldn't believe what he was seeing. When it was all said and done, West Virginia beat us by 28, which was the worst loss I would ever suffer in my collegiate career and was the worst home loss for Ohio State basketball in over 10 years.

The very next day following the West Virginia loss, Noopy requested his scholarship release so he could transfer to another school. Some have suggested that this was because he played only 12 minutes against West Virginia after not getting much playing time in our nine other games (mostly because when he did play he completely and utterly sucked ass). But I know the real reason. Noopy quit because he and I had come to blows just two days earlier, over the same thing that has sparked just about every fight throughout the history of mankind—a rack of baby back ribs from Applebee's.

TWENTY-SIX

As much as I liked to make fun of The Villain for being a head case during his first couple of years at Ohio State, he was nowhere near as crazy as Noopy was. From my perspective, The Villain was more of a case of "it's cute how upset he gets at trivial things," whereas Noopy was "I genuinely fear for my life because he has blown everything out of proportion and is fuming over something that should've never been an issue in the first place." The Villain only got the attention as the mentally unstable guy on the team because he was older and already established as a bit of a nut, but Noopy was borderline psychotic and would ream into teammates on a daily basis for not being able to catch his no-look passes that he rocketed off their ankles or faces. Even with these daily outbursts, I don't think anyone could've anticipated him completely blowing a gasket like he did when he tried to fight me before the West Virginia game.

About a week before the West Virginia game, and the night before the Iona game, we gathered at our arena to take a team bus to a hotel on campus. In case you don't remember from the story earlier in the book about Ivan getting a beej while I was 10 feet from him, let me remind you that it was standard procedure for us to stay in a hotel on campus the night before weekend games as a way to prevent guys from going to parties or bars all night. And to deter guys from sneaking out of the hotel in the middle of the night, it was also standard procedure for us to meet at the arena and take a bus to the hotel to ensure that we wouldn't have our cars waiting for us in the hotel parking lot. Because this meant that we were held captive in the hotel all night, the manager driving the bus would always take us somewhere to get food before he dropped us off. More often than not, we would go to a plaza just north of campus that had both a McDonald's and a Raising Cane's (a chicken finger restaurant that is popular in the South as well as a handful of other places across the country, including Columbus). Also included in this plaza was—you guessed it—an Applebee's.

It was understood that we were to make the process as fast as possible because we all just wanted to get back to the hotel, hang out for a little bit, and then eventually fall asleep (or get a beej with our roommate in the room). Not only that, but our director of basketball operations, Dave Egelhoff, always waited for us at the hotel because he had to be there to check all of us in, so getting our food quickly was kind of the courteous thing to do. The manager driving the bus would just park in between McDonald's and Cane's, and the guys would pick one to get their food from (or just sit in the bus because they planned on getting a pizza delivered once we got to the hotel).

Every now and then, guys would walk to the other end of the plaza to get Subway or even go into the Kroger to get some groceries (I once bought a tub of ice cream to take to the hotel), but they moved quickly and didn't take any more time than the guys who went to McDonald's and Cane's. Simply put, it was understood that we unofficially had about 10 minutes to get our food and get back to the bus. In other words, we clearly didn't have time to go to Applebee's. But on this particular night Will and Noopy had a hankering for some baby back ribs and, rules be damned, nothing was going to stand in their way.

When we parked between McDonald's and Cane's, everyone except Will and Noopy got off the bus, went to one of the two fast-food places, got their food, and promptly returned to the bus. After about 10 minutes of waiting on the bus, we finally realized we had no idea where Will and Noopy were, so one of my teammates texted Will and discovered that they were both waiting for food at Applebee's. I decided to go investigate. When I peeked through a window and saw both of them sitting at the bar with drinks in front of them, I decided that I had seen enough. I returned to the bus and explained the situation to everyone and tried to persuade the manager to drop us all off at the hotel and come back to get Will and Noopy. The manager said he was under strict orders from Egelhoff to not leave until everyone was on the bus, so I had to sit down and wait it out.

After 10 more minutes of waiting, we got impatient and started egging on our manager to leave Will and Noopy and just come back and get them later. He again stressed that he didn't want to get in trouble and suggested that I call Egelhoff to ask him if it would be okay to leave, so I stepped to the plate and took on a leadership role since nobody else on the team would. But right as I got done explaining the situation to Egelhoff over the phone, Will and Noopy came out of Applebee's holding a couple of to-go bags, so I told Egelhoff not to worry about it anymore because we had resolved the situation. When Will and Noopy returned to the bus, I hung up the phone and stopped caring about the whole ordeal because I was just happy that we were finally going to the hotel. This is where I thought the story would end. But sadly, for Noopy the story was just beginning.

A week later, we gathered around Coach Matta after practice to hear his final thoughts on the day's practice and the upcoming game against West Virginia. Following Coach Matta's speech, Egelhoff walked to the middle of the huddle and explained the plans for the evening and told us to meet back at the arena at 8:00 p.m. to go to the hotel, before going on to remind us that when we went to get food before heading to the hotel, we were supposed to get fast food or at the very least get something relatively quick. He then went on to look directly at Noopy and Will and say, "That means no Applebee's."

Everyone in the huddle gave a light chuckle, and we went our **separate ways.** Most of the guys stayed up in the practice gym to get extra shots up, but since I never played and had no desire to get better, I headed straight for the locker room so I could take a shower, change, and go home as soon as possible. And since Noopy preferred bitching about his lack of playing time instead of taking the initiative to put in the extra work and improve his game, he followed right behind.

When I finished showering and made my way back to my locker to get dressed, Noopy was sitting at his locker waiting for me. "That's messed up that you gotta go snitching to Egelhoff," he said and let out what I thought was a playful laugh, but later learned was one of those evil "getting murdered is in your imme- diate future" laughs.

I turned back to Noopy. "Yeah, I wasn't really snitching, though," I said. "I honestly couldn't have cared less what you guys were doing, so it's not like I was trying to tattle to Egelhoff that you were breaking some rules. I just wanted to go to the hotel because I was tired, and the only way that could happen was to explain the situation to Egelhoff. But then you guys came back to the bus, so I told Egelhoff not to worry about it anymore and I hung up on him. It was all just a big misunderstanding. Besides, everyone else was just as impatient as I was. I was just the one who actually made the call."

Noopy had no interest in listening to my reasoning, and he walked toward me with an intense scowl on his face. "Nah, you snitched," he said. "And that's fucked up."

Sensing legitimate anger, I decided the best way to handle the situation was to just laugh it off and pretend he wasn't even there. This might not have been a great idea, because my laughter pissed Noopy off even more and led to him getting in my face.

Now, if you've been paying close attention to this story up to this point, you might be confused about a small detail that I mentioned earlier but haven't addressed since. Well, the answer is yes—I had yet to get dressed after getting out of the shower, meaning I was still butt-ass naked as all of this was happening.

Noopy approached me with clenched fists and tears welling in his eyes, and he said, "Don't laugh, bitch. This shit's not funny. You were trying to get me in trouble 'cause you're a snitch."

Since fighting him was completely out of the question for a variety of reasons (I was naked, he was clearly more worked up than me so his adrenaline would've been a huge advantage for him, and it's a personal policy of mine to not throw down in fisticuffs over baby back ribs), I decided to try to use my nakedness to my advantage and diffuse the situation the only logical way I saw fit.

Most of the guys on the team were some of the biggest homophobes on the planet, so I thought that my pork sword just flopping around out in the open would be my best defense and would successfully deter Noopy from starting a physical altercation. I made good use of my exposed wiener by saying to Noopy, "Just calm down. You know I don't like it when you get angry. Look, every time you get all worked up like this, it makes me flaccid."

This didn't exactly work as planned. Noopy shoved me into the wall with both hands and yelled, "This isn't a fucking joke!" Whoops.

A couple of teammates walked into the locker room and surely misinterpreted the sight of Noopy trying to pin my naked body up against a wall while he and I were the only two in the room. Upon realizing that Noopy wasn't aggressively in the process of performing fellatio on me but was instead moments away from trying to beat me senseless, they rushed over to break everything up. Noopy shoved me again, whiffed on what would've been a powerful punch to my face, dropped a bunch of F-bombs, and repeatedly alternated between calling me a "bitch" and a "snitch."

After my teammates restrained Noopy, I got dressed and had to laugh at how ridiculous it was that Noopy wanted to brawl because I didn't have the patience to sit on a cramped and crowded bus for 20 minutes while he selfishly got baby back ribs. Even funnier was the fact that every other guy on the team felt the same way I did, so if Noopy was going to have a beef, it should've been with everyone else too. Anyway, I finished getting dressed, walked out of the locker room, went home, and to this day have still not spoken a single word to Noopy since the incident.

Two days later Noopy had transferred, and we all gathered in the locker room to reflect on his brief stint at Ohio State. I rather predictably bragged about how I was responsible for making him quit, which prompted a surprise reaction from some of my teammates. Much like how I was chastised by my teammates when The Villain lost his cool in a practice the year before (the practice where he tried to punch me because I asked him to throw me a bounce pass), some of my teammates criticized *me* for Noopy's actions. They claimed that I "should have known better than to laugh" and that I "had to have known that he was going to snap."

While that may be true, the fact of the matter is that if I actually did snitch, I also snitched on Will, yet he never once said anything to me about it and never had a problem with me (another example of why Will is my all-time favorite teammate), so clearly I wasn't the problem and clearly the entire issue should've never gotten to the point where I even had the opportunity to laugh at Noopy for getting mad. Either way, this will go down as one of my favorite memories of my time at Ohio State, if for no other reason than it's fun to reduce the whole ordeal to just "Noopy tried to fight me over baby back ribs from Applebee's."

Also, it is memorable for me because, as unbelievable as it may sound, this was only the first of three different times throughout that season that a teammate of mine instigated an altercation with me while I was naked. You can read into that whatever you want, but as far as I'm concerned this trend is obvious proof that guys on the team would notice just how enormous my dong was as I got out of the shower and then would try to fight me because my massive man meat made them jealous and insecure.

TWENTY-SEVEN

After losing Dave for the season shortly before the West Virginia beat-down, and then dealing with Noopy's exodus from the team shortly thereafter, we were at a crisis point right as our first conference game was upon us. Luckily, we opened the Big Ten season against a pretty bad Iowa team at home. But Iowa was 10–3 coming into the game, and since they had beaten up on a bunch of cupcake teams for the first half of the season, they weren't yet aware that they actually kinda sucked.

We controlled most of the first half and took an eight-point lead into halftime, but Iowa came storming back when the second half started and tied the game before the first media time-out. We responded with a mini-run of our own and briefly led by seven, but Iowa showed a ton of resilience and kept the game close the rest of the way. In the end, we squeaked out a three-point win that was one of those wins that could be interpreted as either "this is just what we needed to get back on track" or "there is serious cause for concern because we should have blown these guys out." Judging from our results in the immediate future, it was the latter.

Following the close win against Iowa, we lost by nine at 21st-ranked Minnesota in what was certainly an unmemorable game. But even though the game wasn't anything to write home about (and let's be honest—with today's technology, I don't think anybody is writing home about anything anymore), the entire road trip itself was probably my favorite of my career. That's because, thanks to a series of paranoid, mean-spirited, and just flat-out dumb events, I got stuck on an elevator with two of my teammates and our trainer for over an hour.

Since the blog post I originally wrote a few years ago about this incident seemed to be the consensus favorite among people who followed my blog, I figure I'll stick with the same retroactive diary format for the book that I used back then. And by that I mean that I have basically just copied and pasted the blog post into this book. But if you are one of the people who read the original that was posted in January 2009, don't you worry—I did a good deal of editing, so really it's not the same story but just resembles the original story and is now much better. (I guess this is the same thing the people behind Disney's version of *Doug* thought too.)

Besides, even if it was the exact same, it won't kill you to reread it. Unless, of course, you're reading it again while driving a car or operating a flamethrower or something. Then you might be screwed.

Anyway, here's how everything went down:

6:07 p.m.—We return to the hotel from practice at Minnesota's gym and are informed that we are watching film in 30 minutes. I make a mental note that this is more than enough time for me to pull a prank on The Villain. Ideas start flowing.

6:09 p.m.—I get off the bus and make my way to the hotel lobby to wait for an elevator to take me up to my room. I've got my headphones on, and I'm listening to Alan Jackson's "Livin' on Love," even though I have an intense scowl on my face that I'm hoping portrays to onlookers that I'm a badass who listens to heavy metal or hard-core rap. The nerdy kid from *The Little Giants* would no doubt be impressed with this intimidation tactic.

6:12 p.m.—An elevator finally arrives, and a group of about six players get on board, including Walter Offutt, Will Buford, and myself. I turn my music off because I don't want my teammates to overhear my sappy country music and make fun of me. Will, however, leaves his music on and is listening to some rapper I have never heard of and bobs his body up and down. Apparently bobbing up and down is Will's method of dancing along with his music, which I find particularly interesting considering he's the same guy who always claimed that I was a terrible dancer. (Bobbing up and down versus copious hip thrusting and "suck it" crotch chops—you tell me which is the better form of dancing.) Will continues to dance, and Walter has a Don Vito moment as he gets so upset and starts yelling so quickly it's difficult to understand what he's actually trying to say.

As a guy with a history of paranoia and all sorts of phobias, Walter apparently isn't too thrilled with Will making the elevator shake. He tries to get off the elevator, but a few of the other guys notice how worried he is and try to hold him back because tormenting Walter is their way of showing brotherly love. But Walter's adrenaline kicks in, and he punches, scratches, and claws his way toward the elevator door. In his desperation to escape, he resembles a cornered animal or a girl being hit on by Ben Roethlisberger.

He eventually sticks his arm into the door frame of the elevator and prevents the door from closing, before finally walking off the elevator. I notice that even though he is off the elevator and free from danger, he is still visibly upset. I realize this is a perfect opportunity to exploit his weakened mental state, and I exit the elevator with him. This seems like a good time to mention that I have a video camera with me and plan on recording some good footage of Walter losing his mind.

6:15 p.m.—The next elevator comes. Walter, Danny, our trainer Vince O'Brien, and I board. Danny pushes the button to take us to the 18th floor while Walter, still upset by the scare that Will gave him, silently hangs out in the corner of the elevator with a disgruntled look on his face. I go in for the kill.

6:16 p.m.—I turn the video camera on and point it in Walter's direction. "Walter, why were you so scared on that last elevator?" I ask, even though I know exactly why he was so scared.

" 'Cause I can't stand it when people be jumping on elevators!"

As predictable as Walter's response was, though, it isn't nearly as predictable as what happens next. As soon as Walter finishes talking and the doors to the elevator close, Danny says, "You mean like this, Walter?" as he launches himself into the air and stomps his feet when he lands, a lot like Diamond Dallas Page used to do when he'd walk out of the tunnel after being introduced, throw up his diamond hand signal thing, and then stomp on the ground as pyrotechnics exploded all around him. (On second thought, that makes Danny seem much more badass than he actually is, so forget I ever made the DDP comparison.)

Walter starts yelling at the top of his lungs. I am laughing hysterically and have the camera focused on Walter. I decide to join the fun and start bobbing my body a little bit (although it should be noted that my bobbing is nowhere near the intensity of Danny's jumping). Vince also gets in on the action and bobs up and down even less than I am. Not long after Vince starts bobbing, Danny lands from one of his ill-advised jumps and the elevator starts shaking. The elevator then stops on what appears to be the ninth floor. The doors do not open. We are stuck.

6:17 p.m.—To say that Walter is pissed when he realizes that we are stuck on the elevator and one of his biggest fears is suddenly a reality would be a bigger understatement than saying that the Indian kid with the "heart" ring on *Captain Planet* got an unfair deal when those magical rings were distributed. He is now so insane that it honestly wouldn't have been much of a surprise to me if he started dancing around in his grandma's panties and rubbed himself in peanut butter.

Luckily, he yells mostly at Danny, but he also directs a little bit of his hatred toward me. Even though Walter's anger has me genuinely fearing for my life, I can't help but laugh because this particular outburst is by far the most intense (and therefore the most comical) of all of his outbursts from throughout the year. Making it that much better is the fact that I'm documenting the entire ordeal with my video camera.

6:18 p.m.—I realize I forgot to hit the Record button on the camera. I am now almost as upset as Walter. I hit Record and hope to at least get some solid post-freak-out footage.

6:20 p.m.—Walter is cooling down a little bit, but is still very upset. At this point he's going with the silent angry approach, just like Othello did when we were on the plane coming back from Penn State and we hit that patch of turbulence. Danny is trying to justify the fact that he basically did a series of cannonballs in an elevator and suggests that it was the elevator's fault for not being sturdy enough. He also tries to place equal parts of the blame on Vince and me.

Meanwhile, Vince is sitting down in one of the corners of the elevator and is surprisingly taking the situation well. To further screw with Walter, I decide to turn the camera on myself and do a *Blair Witch Project* parody by tilting my head back, zooming in on my nostrils, and pretending to be seriously concerned that we might not make it out of the elevator alive even though we've been trapped for four minutes. Walter isn't amused.

6:22 p.m.—We decide it would be a good idea to utilize the emergency phone in the elevator. Danny calls the front desk to the hotel and explains the situation. Danny leaves out the part about him doing a swanton bomb onto the floor of the elevator. Probably a wise decision on his part.

6:25 p.m.—I bring up the idea of cannibalism and ask for a volunteer to be the first to be eaten. No takers. Vince then declares that he has nutrition bars in his trainer bag. I think about the consequences of turning to cannibalism within 10 minutes of getting stuck in the elevator and decide it's probably best to just eat a nutrition bar.

6:29 p.m.—Walter pulls out his cell phone and calls somebody to discuss the situation. I ask him who he is talking to and he says his girlfriend. I respond with, "Is this the same one from last night?" loud enough for her to hear me. Walter flips out again and explains to his woman that it was just a joke.

6:34 p.m.—I eyeball the top of the elevator and think about a possible escape by climbing out of the elevator and down the elevator shaft. Walter is still talking to his girlfriend explaining that I was only kidding about him being with another girl. Danny is texting various people on both his "work phone" and his "phone for the ladies." Yes, you read that right—Danny has two cell phones and refers to one as a work phone (even though he's a college basketball player and in no way has enough time for a real job) and the other as his phone for the girls he talks to. (More than anything else, that's all you need to know about Danny.)

I approach Vince and ask him to tape my ankles for added support during the escape. Sure it might sound crazy to get my ankles taped, but I can't help but think how badly it would suck if I somehow slipped during the escape, fell 90 feet down an elevator shaft, and tweaked my ankle as I landed at the bottom. Safety always comes first.

6:37 p.m.—The film session is supposed to have started. I don't feel quite as badly as I should that I'm missing it.

6:40 p.m.—As I'm preparing to make my escape, I remember that the two most popular places in hotels for serial killers to stash their victims' bodies are in the shower of the victim's room or on the roof of an elevator à la Hannibal Lecter. I decide that the possibility of opening the hatch on the ceiling of the elevator and having a dead dude without a face fall down is too much of a risk for me to try it, especially considering I had priors and the cops would have surely thought I was somehow involved. I opt to wait it out instead.

6:42 p.m.—I rewind the video I recorded and begin watching it to pass the time. Walter is still a little distraught, so he calls the front desk lady back on the emergency phone and makes small talk with her. He begins telling her stories about his basketball career that date all the way back to when he was in junior high. I find this conversation he is having worthy of recording on the video camera, so I stop the tape I am watching and begin recording Walter again.

6:45 p.m.—Walter asks the lady at the front desk, "You think we can get some pizzas or something since your elevators broke on us?" He then goes on to order pizzas for everyone in the elevator. Right before he hangs up, he says, "Thanks for those pizzas. We'll call back in 10 minutes with more demands." Danny explains to Walter that we aren't holding anybody hostage and "we'll call back with more demands" was probably a poor choice of words.

6:51 p.m.—I realize that by rewinding the videotape earlier and not fast-forwarding it back to the end when I started recording again, I recorded over all the footage I had previously taken. My inability to operate a video camera is now becoming annoying to everyone in the elevator.

6:53 p.m.—I put the camera back on Walter and ask him if he has anything to say for the camera. He begins talking to the camera as if it represents all of his loved ones by saying things like "Just want you to know that I love you, Mom, and I'm going to find a way out of here, I promise." This gives me an idea. I suggest to Walter that he should make a video to play at his funeral in case we don't make it out of the elevator. This sets him off again and makes him yell at me to stop talking about the possibility of us dying.

6:54 p.m.—Since Walter has no interest in doing it, I decide to make a mock video for my funeral, mostly because I know it will drive Walter insane. For the first time since this whole ordeal started, I question whether or not I'm being too mean to Walter, but in the end I decide that, just like with Othello on the plane, this is something we'll all think back on and laugh about someday. (Luckily, unlike Othello, Walter does laugh about it now.)

6:59 p.m.—Walter calls back the lady at the front desk. She claims help is on the way and we'll be rescued soon, which is the exact same thing she said 30 minutes ago. I ask Walter to put in a good word for me and to ask her what color of panties she is wearing. He does neither. I guess this is his way of paying me back. Walter instead asks her for a free iPhone because he claims his iPhone somehow was destroyed when the elevator broke down. Walter doesn't even have an iPhone to begin with, and the phone he does have is obviously not broken. I can't hear what her response is, but seeing as how Walter goes on to say, "I was just messing witchu, I'm sorry," I'm guessing she has no plans to get Walter a free iPhone. I realize at this point that there is no way in hell the people on the outside are doing all they can to rescue us after Walter's spectacular performance on the phone.

7:05 p.m.—A call comes in to Vince from Egelhoff. He explains to Vince that the team meal is almost over and if we want any food we should hurry up and get out of the elevator. Vince explains that we aren't on the elevator by choice. And even if we were, we didn't need the team meal because Walter brilliantly negotiated some free pizzas from the hotel staff.

7:15 p.m.—After about an hour of being stuck, the elevator finally starts moving. We drop down to the eighth floor. I push Walter out of the way so I can get a good shot of the welcoming party that is surely waiting on us. I'm envisioning banners, balloons, confetti, news cameras, and an oversized card signed with sloppy cursive by an entire elementary school waiting for us right outside the elevator. Basically, I'm expecting the equivalent of a soldier's homecoming party. This doesn't seem like too much to ask.

7:17 p.m.—The door is still yet to open. I turn my camera off to conserve battery for the actual rescue. As soon as I power down the camera and begin putting it away, the door opens and the only person I see is a middle-aged lady with a name tag that reads Bernice. Walter asks if she is the lady we were talking to on the emergency phone in the elevator. Bernice confirms that she is. I immediately regret my request to ask for the color of her underpants.

7:18 p.m.—Danny texts one of our coaches and asks what the team is doing. The coach says they're about to start the film session. Danny relays the information to me, at which point I kindly ask him if he is shitting me. Danny confirms that he is not in fact shitting me and that the team really did delay the film session just for us.

To give you a proper analogy, this is the equivalent of your wife saying, "My friend really wants to go to the ballet with me, but I told her I couldn't give her my extra ticket because I figured you would want to go." *You mean to tell me that a legitimate opportunity to get out of something I despise presented itself, but you screwed everything up because you thought you were doing me a favor? Sonofabitch.*

7:21 p.m.—We arrive at the film room. I rack my brain for ideas on how I can avoid having to sit through an hour of film after spending the past hour stuck in a crammed elevator. Ultimately, I realize that if getting stuck in the elevator wasn't going to get me out of film, nothing was. Damn.

7:56 p.m.—We get out of film and two large pizza boxes are waiting. One has Walter's name on it, and the other has my name on it. Danny is furious that his pizza is missing. Danny calls Vince, and Vince tells him that he also got his pizza. Apparently, Danny is the only one of the four that didn't get any pizza. Sucks to be him.

8:05 p.m.—Danny and I return to our room. I'm devouring my pizza in front of Danny. I explain to him how karma works, and Danny is not amused in the slightest. He calls the front desk asking for his pizza. The lady at the front desk claims she ordered one for him and placed it outside the film room. Danny swears his pizza was stolen, but I think the lady knew all along that it was his fault the elevator got stuck and "forgot" to get a fourth pizza for him. Either way, my pizza is delicious and I'm not sharing.

TWENTY-EIGHT

After our Minnesota loss, we went on the road to play eighth-ranked Michigan State in East Lansing, where we ended up losing by nine despite outscoring the Spartans in the second half. It was certainly an excusable loss considering we played pretty well and Michigan State was one of the best teams in the country that year, but now that we were 1–3 since our captain (Dave) went down with a foot injury (and 1–2 since one of our players quit after trying to fight me when I was naked), it was obvious that we were in a state of turmoil. We needed to get back on track, and we needed to get back on track fast. Thankfully, our next two games were against an atrocious Houston Baptist team and an only slightly better Indiana team. But just a few weeks after we lost our team captain for the rest of the season, our bad luck continued when the face of the program and our team's best player fractured his foot in practice and was declared out for six weeks.

To be honest, I don't remember a whole lot of specifics about the circumstances of my foot injury. (What's that? You didn't think I was talking about myself when I said "face of the program" and "team's best player"? Shame on you.) All I really remember is that Dallas tried to block my layup attempt and all 250 pounds of him came down right on my foot as I was rolling my ankle, causing the most physical pain I had ever felt in my life. I also remember the next morning when I rolled out of bed, took one step toward the bathroom to take my routine morning pee, and then instantly collapsed to the floor as intense pain shot up my leg.

At practice later that day, Vince examined my foot and told me that I probably had a Lisfranc (pronounced "Liz Frank") fracture, which prompted me to ask if it was named that because that Jewish chick with the diary hurt her foot while trying to hide from the Nazis. He responded by telling me that the injury was actually named after a French gynecologist for some reason, which was proof to him that I didn't hurt my foot but instead must have hurt my vagina. Touché. Either way, I had a hairline fracture on the top of my foot and was suddenly even more useless to the team than I had been, which was something that I had always thought was an impossibility.

As I'm sure you could have guessed, my absence didn't really have much of an effect on the team, as evidenced by the fact that we basically told both Houston Baptist and Indiana to shut up and make us a sandwich en route to two 24-point wins. Those two blowouts were then followed up with a seven-point win in Ann Arbor against 24th-ranked Michigan, which gave us our first significant win since Dave (and I) got hurt. Unfortunately, though, our elation was short-lived, because just three days after the Michigan win we were blown out at 24th-ranked Illinois and then lost by 11 to seventh-ranked Michigan State in our rematch with them at home, dropping our record to just 4–5 since Dave got hurt.

But just as it seemed as though we were never going to figure out how to gel without Dave (or me), we went on a tear and rattled off four straight wins, with the first two coming in the form of an 18-point mushroom-stamping of Michigan at home and a blowout of Indiana at their place. To complete our streak, we squeaked out an overtime thriller against 12th-ranked Purdue at home and followed that up with another big home win against 19th-ranked Minnesota. And with that, we were feeling pretty good about ourselves because we were playing our best basketball of the season and had finally proven that we could win big games without Dave. More importantly, on a personal level, I was not only happy that we were playing well, but also pretty pleased that none of my teammates had tried to fight me in quite some time. It wouldn't take long for The Villain to change this, though.

Shortly after the Minnesota game, my foot was declared to be fully healed, and I was cleared to start practicing again. But within the first five minutes of my first practice back, Dallas, honest to God, landed on the exact same foot he had injured six weeks earlier, which forced me to make my comeback a little bit slower than I was originally planning. I timidly eased my way back into practice and eventually started participating in live contact drills about a week later, which was perfect timing considering we lost a close game at Wisconsin just days earlier and my comeback, I thought, would surely galvanize the team to make sure the singular loss didn't turn into another losing streak. Only instead of being excited to see me making it rain on the practice court again, most of the guys on the team were indifferent to my return, and some didn't even have any idea that I had been hurt in the first place. The Villain, though, was the one exception who was no doubt thrilled to see me practicing again, as evidenced by the fact that he had to be restrained by a group of my teammates because he tried to instigate yet another in-practice fight between us.

The genesis of this particular altercation came when I somehow found myself on the court during a scrimmage at the end of practice in which my team was up by two with the ball and there was less than a minute on the clock. For whatever reason, The Villain (by far the best player on the court) was guarding me for this critical possession, most likely because he remembered my late game practice heroics from the year before, when I hit the three at the buzzer to send our scrimmage into overtime (and Jamar proceeded to get four technicals and ruin everything), and he wanted to embrace the challenging assignment of shutting The Shark down in crunch time. This time around, though, I was confident that I would not be called upon to do anything because not only was I considered the worst player on my team, but I also was just getting back from a serious foot injury and was therefore even worse than I usually was. (I can't even begin to guess why I'm on the court in the first place in these situations.) But obviously, I wouldn't be telling this story if I just stood out of the way and didn't do anything.

As the shot clock ticked down to about eight seconds, whoever had the ball on my team started dribbling toward me, so I cut toward the basket and ran to the opposite corner because it served the dual function of getting out of the way and making it seem as though I was legitimately trying to make something happen (even though I wasn't). My teammate interpreted this cut as the latter instead of the former and immediately passed the ball to another teammate at the top of the key, who then swung the ball to me in the corner. In both of these guys' defense, I did create some separation from The Villain and might have been able to get a shot off had I shot the ball as soon as I caught it. But even so, as a general rule of thumb, passing me the ball with a dwindling shot clock under any circumstances is a recipe for disaster.

Nonetheless, as I caught the ball I couldn't help but think that it might be the only time in my entire basketball career at Ohio State that I would have carte blanche. Since the shot clock was winding down, I would have been completely justified in taking pretty much any shot I wanted. I could have shot a left-handed fadeaway or a running hook shot, or just thrown the ball over my head with my back to the basket if I wanted. My coaches would have been fine with truly any shot, because with just six seconds left on the shot clock, it was clear that the one decision that had already been made for me was that I had no choice but to shoot the ball.

I decided to disregard the safe play and bypass the initial shot I would have had if I'd let it fly as soon as I caught it, and instead chose to back The Villain down into the post to feed him a heaping helping of fundamentals. Now, intuition would tell you that this was a terrible idea on my part because The Villain was bigger, faster, stronger, more athletic, and generally just much more talented than me. You would think that I should have just shot the ball while I had the chance instead of letting The Villain get in a comfortable defensive position. But what you're failing to realize is that I had a leg up on The Villain in a couple of other areas, namely basketball (and overall) IQ and my ability to tie balloon animals. On this particular play, though, I would only need to utilize one of those strengths.

Once I backed The Villain all the way down to the right block, the shot clock showed just four seconds, so I knew I'd have to make my move quickly. Like pretty much every other time I have the ball during a scrimmage or game, I thought to myself, *What would Larry Bird do?* and decided that he would have surely tried to make The Villain look foolish by using a pump-fake somehow, so that's what I went for. I took two dribbles toward the middle of the lane, pushed off my right foot, picked up my dribble as I jumped back toward the free throw line to create separation and make it look like I was about to shoot a fadeaway, and sold the fake so well that even I thought I was about to shoot it.

The Villain knew that the shot clock buzzer was about to go off, figured my fake was a desperation shot, and threw his entire body in the air and stretched out his arm to block it. As he soared through the air with just one second left on the shot clock, I tried to step under his outstretched body and lay the ball in the basket, except, as I went to do this, I saw The Villain's knee heading right toward my face. (I still don't know if he was trying to knee me in the face on purpose or not.) At the last instant, I ducked out of the way, slightly bent over to avoid getting a mouthful of his knee, and blindly threw the ball toward the basket. As that happened, The Villain rolled over the top of my back and landed hard on his hip to the sound of an echoing thud and a blowing whistle.

Foul on The Villain. Two free throws for The Shark. Larry Legend would've no doubt been proud.

Almost instantly after he hit the deck, The Villain sprang back up and came charging toward me, but was held back by a few teammates. (Apparently he was pissed because he thought I intentionally tried to hurt him or something.) As they tried to calm him down, I turned my back to him and tried my best to ignore him while I lined up for my free throws. Eventually, he calmed down enough to where he wasn't a threat to physically attack me, but he certainly didn't calm down enough to refrain from calling me a "punk-ass bitch" and warning me that "if you try that shit again I'll knock your ass out" while I sank both of my free throws and sealed the scrimmage win for our team.

After practice, I stayed in the gym for a little bit because I figured The Villain would try to fight me in the locker room and I wanted to give him a second to cool down. After I sat down and started taking my shoes off, Coach Matta approached me with a grave look on his face and said, "Mark, if you ever pull a stunt like that again, your ass is gone. I just can't have that on my basketball team. I mean, to have the audacity to make the smart basketball play and pump-fake the almighty Evan Turner? I won't stand for it. You're better than that."

I breathed a sigh of relief when, halfway through, he cracked a smile that turned into straight-up laughter. In fact, from what I was told by a handful of different players and managers, as everything was unfolding Coach Matta actually covered his face with the sheet of paper in his hand because he was turning red from laughing so hard at The Villain. I can't say for sure, but I'm pretty confident this marked the first time in history that a walk-on undercut his superstar teammate and caused him to violently land on the floor and the head coach not only sided with the walk-on but actually turned red from laughing so hard at the superstar. So that's something to be proud of.

Two days after The Villain fell victim to my silky smooth post moves and consequently tried to fight me, we played at Northwestern and he guarded Northwestern's Kevin Coble, who was one of the best players in the Big Ten that season. At some point during the game, Coble caught the ball on the right wing and—I shit you not—proceeded to back The Villain down to the right block before he took a couple of dribbles toward the lane, pump-faked, and went to the free throw line after The Villain bit on the fake and hammered him. It was the exact same play that I executed in practice, only now, since we were on TV in primetime and it was one of the Big Ten's best players who did it instead of me, The Villain kept his mouth shut and solemnly walked away from Coble. Vindication never tasted so sweet to me.

He'll never admit it, but I'd be willing to bet that, as he watched Coble shoot the free throws, The Villain cursed my name under his breath because he knew that I was getting so much enjoyment not only out of seeing him fall for the exact same move that I got him on, but also seeing him puss out of confronting Coble when he was so anxious to fight me. And make no mistake about it—I was getting a ton of enjoyment out of it. I laughed to myself for damn near the rest of the game and only stopped laughing when Northwestern hit a last-second three and beat us for the only time during my four-year career.

TWENTY-NINE

ollowing the loss to Northwestern, we were completely outplayed at home by 16th-ranked Illinois and lost by two in a
game that we never led and that we never were much of a
threat to win despite keeping the score close all game. With the
loss, we were now in the middle of a three-game losing streak,
which was our worst losing streak of the season but wasn't cause
for too much concern because we lost those three games only by a
combined 10 points. Thankfully, we bounced back with a win over
Penn State at home, but turned right around and got completely
mutilated in a 25-point loss to Purdue at their place. Whereas
most of our other losses throughout the season were either close
or semi-justifiable, a blowout loss to a Purdue team that we had
beaten earlier in the season was nothing short of an inexcusable
embarrassment. With only two games left in the regular season,
it wasn't exactly a great time in the season to be getting our asses
handed to us like that.

After Purdue we played Iowa, who we coincidentally played
immediately after we were blown out by West Virginia earlier in

the season. And much like that first matchup with the Hawkeyes, this time around we also continued our poor play from the previous game and let the game get much closer than it probably should have been. Luckily, though, in the end we were able to escape Iowa City with a two-point win after a game-winning three-point attempt from Iowa at the buzzer clanked off the rim.

An interesting note from this game (and by "interesting" I mean "pretty disgusting") is that, with about eight minutes left, I felt an overwhelming surge of diarrhea knocking on my butthole, letting me know that it was on the precipice of making a serious mess in my underpants. Because of the way Iowa's gym was structured, I couldn't go back to our locker room without drawing attention to myself by walking in front of Iowa's bench, so I held it in for the remainder of the game. (If I'd gone during the last media time-out, I'd have been stuck because I would've had to walk back in front of Iowa's bench as the game was going on to get back to my spot on our bench.)

After eight excruciating minutes of waiting, as soon as the buzzer sounded I shook hands with all of Iowa's players, darted straight to the locker room, and relieved myself while Coach Matta gave his postgame speech to the team just a few yards away. I then proceeded to remain on the toilet for no less than 45 minutes to finish my business. When I finally completed the task at hand, I walked out of the stall and was greeted by the sight of an empty locker room, so I quickly changed out of my uniform, gathered all my stuff together, and ran to our bus, where I discovered that everyone on the team had been waiting for me for at least 10 minutes. I'd be lying if I said I wasn't much more proud than I was apologetic.

After the close Iowa win quite literally scared the crap out of me, we closed out the regular season with yet another close one at home against Northwestern. These last two wins clinched the five seed in the Big Ten Tournament for us, where we were to face the fourth-seeded Wisconsin Buzzcuts in our opening-round game. They had already beaten us that season, so we were out for a little revenge and ultimately were able to get that revenge when we pulled away late and beat them by four.

With the win over the Buzzcuts, we advanced to play top-seeded and sixth-ranked Michigan State in the next round. Michigan State entered the game as a candidate for a number-one seed in the NCAA Tournament, so they had a lot to play for. But like Donny Kerabatsos and a child who wanders into the middle of a movie, they surprisingly looked completely out of their element. We led for pretty much the entire game and won by 12. This win set up the grudge match against third-seeded Purdue for the Big Ten Tournament Championship, but Purdue had more gas in the tank down the stretch and beat us by four.

Even though we let the final game slip away, we still had a pretty strong run through the Big Ten Tournament (highlighted by beating one of the best teams in the country) and removed all doubt as to whether we'd get a bid to the NCAA Tournament. The only questions that remained were what seed we'd get, who we'd play, and whether or not someone on our team would poop his pants right before our pregame shootaround. As we'd soon find out, the answers to these questions were, respectively, eight, Siena, and, unfortunately, yes.

Immediately after the Big Ten Championship game, we gathered as a team in a room at Conseco Fieldhouse to watch the *NCAA Tournament Selection Show*, during which Greg Gumbel informed us that we had been given an eight seed and were to play ninth-seeded Siena in Dayton for our first-round game. Most of us were less concerned about Siena and more concerned about the fact that after we beat Siena we were most likely going to have to play our second-round game against Louisville, who was the number-one overall seed for the entire tournament and had been pretty dominant all season. This is what we in the business refer to as "looking ahead," and it's typically never a good thing. ("Looking ahead" shouldn't be confused with foreshadowing, which is what I just did by saying we were more concerned about Louisville than Siena, and then just did again by explicitly stating that I was foreshadowing.) But as bad of a feeling as I got, it was nothing compared to the bad vibes I got when we boarded the team bus to go to our morning shootaround on the day of the game and The Villain was nowhere to be found.

Fifteen minutes after we were supposed to have left to go to our shootaround, The Villain finally boarded the bus with a huge smile across his face that said, "I just did something embarrassing, and this smile is my way of both laughing at myself and overcompensating so none of you think anything is wrong." Most of us could tell something was off, but we couldn't really decipher the message his smile was sending until a teammate stepped in and translated for us. Apparently, while The Villain was on the hotel elevator on his way down to the first floor to get on the bus for the shootaround, he suddenly got quiet and had a look on his face that conveyed that he had just had a terrible realization, kinda like how you'd look in those first couple seconds after you realize that you were supposed to work today or that you forgot to lock your doors before you left for vacation.

Basically, the expression on his face said, *Oh shit*, which, coincidentally, was exactly the problem. According to The Villain, he had been battling a cold for a few days and was given some specific meds from our trainer that produced loose bowels as a side effect. I've had numerous colds in my life and taken all sorts of medications yet have never had loose bowels, so I was a little skeptical about his excuse. Even if he did have loose bowels, I saw no reason why he couldn't have at least anticipated the poop coming and hurried to a bathroom to take care of it. Regardless of who or what is to blame, the fact of the matter is that The Villain boarded the elevator with a fresh pair of underwear on, but when the elevator started to descend, so did the brownie batter.

Now, I don't know specifics about this incident, which is to say that I don't know how big of a mess The Villain actually made, so I can't really gauge exactly how embarrassing this should be for him. Some have speculated that he simply sharted himself, which is embarrassing, sure, but certainly isn't entirely uncommon. (After all, accidentally sharting from time to time is the one common denominator among all of us humans.) I've heard other rumors that it was a full-on dump that he unloaded in his britches, which would be the most embarrassing possibility for him but is also pretty unrealistic. (Although with The Villain nothing is ever truly unrealistic.) The truth is probably somewhere in the middle, but it really doesn't matter to me. What matters is that, no matter how you slice it, the best player on our team and the future National Player of the Year in college basketball pooped his pants before the first NCAA Tournament game of his life and then went out and damn near put up a triple-double as he recorded 25 points, 9 rebounds, and 8 assists.

Not only that, but he did it in the most thrilling game of the entire tournament: our game with Siena went into double overtime, and 17 total points were scored in the final minute of regulation, the final minute of the first overtime, and the final minute of the second overtime combined. In other words, clutch shot after clutch shot was being made, but unfortunately, Siena (read: Siena's Ronald Moore) ended up hitting one more clutch shot than we did and beat us by two to end our season. Making the loss sting that much more was the fact that we held late leads at each closing stage of the game (end of regulation and both overtimes), and each time Siena hit a late shot to either tie or win the game. We still had a chance to win at the end of regulation and both overtimes, but all three would-be game-winners clanked off the rim.

So, to recap, all we needed was one out of three buzzer beaters to go down to win. We got none. If you ask me, that's—pun absolutely intended—a pretty shitty way to end a season.

THIRTY

Following my junior season at Ohio State, BJ Mullens (who had just finished his freshman season) declared for the NBA draft and casually brought up in conversation that it would be funny if I declared too. After giving it some thought (and by "some thought" I mean virtually no thought at all), I realized that this was a perfect idea. Not only was it something I had always kind of wanted to do just to see what would happen, but I also figured it would make for some good entertainment on my blog if I tried to get invited to predraft camps and workouts.

As far as I knew, anyone could put their name in the draft—it was actually getting drafted that was the tricky part. I knew that I wasn't going to get drafted, so the plan was to submit my name for a month or so, try to weasel my way into some workouts and camps, and then remove myself from the draft before the deadline so I could stay eligible for my senior season at Ohio State. I asked BJ what he had to do to officially submit his name, and he told me that Egelhoff gave him some papers to fill out and sign, and then they faxed those papers to the league office in New York.

So, the next day I went to Egelhoff's office and told him I wanted to enter my name into the NBA draft, and he laughed and gave me the papers. Once I wrote down all the pertinent information, he hit a few buttons on the fax machine and sent the papers to the NBA. And with that, I had officially declared myself eligible for the 2009 NBA draft.

A little over a week later, I was working out (shocking, I know) in our practice gym, when Egelhoff opened the doors and walked straight toward me with papers in his hand. He stood about a foot away from me while I was in the middle of a timed shooting drill and said, "The NBA is pissed. Sign these now."

A couple of days earlier, an assistant coach told me that the NBA had called the Ohio State basketball office a few times and told them I was making a mockery of their process, but I assumed he was joking. But now that Egelhoff was urgently shoving papers in my face that appeared to be the papers I was supposed to submit to withdraw my name from the draft, I realized that the NBA wasn't nearly as amused as I was. Even though I didn't technically have to sign the papers, I figured the charade had run its course and I didn't want to tarnish the relationship between the NBA and Ohio State, so I obliged and signed.

After I was forced to remove my name from the draft, I took to my blog to explain what happened. I said "it was fun while it lasted" and explained that I wasn't that upset because I was going to remove my name eventually anyway, so to be the first guy kicked out of the draft was actually an accomplishment I was proud of. Technically and legally speaking, I wasn't actually forced out of the draft, but I pretty much had to sign the papers that were shoved in my face lest I deal with some sort of repercussions . . . so for all intents and purposes I was forced out.

I thought that the blog post would serve as a natural ending to my draft experiment, but I couldn't have been more wrong. Almost instantly after I published my blog post, the ordeal became a huge national story, to the point that it was one of four feature stories on Yahoo.com's home page (along with a story about Barack Obama, a story about Michelle Obama, and a story about the flu outbreak in America), and it was the second-most-searched topic on Google for the day.

Some people were outraged with the NBA, and in the comments section of one article I actually indirectly sparked a race war because a handful of ignorant white guys claimed that I was kicked out just because I was white, a handful of black guys disagreed, and things snowballed from there. A few people emailed me and tried to persuade me to sue the NBA. Others thought I should go to the draft and walk up onstage when an absentee draft pick's name was announced. Everyone I talked to had an opinion on how I should handle the situation, all of them oblivious to the fact that I honestly did not care about getting kicked out and was perfectly fine with it because it worked out much better for me than it would have had I been able to stay eligible for the draft for an extra couple of weeks.

Meanwhile, as everyone around me seemed to be completely enraged, I sat back and laughed at the irony of the situation: the NBA had made me take my name out because they claimed I was making a mockery of their draft, yet by forcing me out they had made the process more of a mockery than I could've ever possibly done on my own.

PART SIX

If you don't know who Mark Titus is, you should be put in juvie.

—*Robbie Fiscus, my then-eight-year-old neighbor*

THIRTY-ONE

A note from the author: Let me first admit and warn you up-front that this will undoubtedly be the douchiest section of the entire book, since it's the part that will leave many of you thinking I'm a conceited dickwad. That's because this section discusses the rise in popularity of my blog and all the notoriety that came with it. But before you flip ahead, you should know that it's not what you think. I'm not writing this section as a way of boasting. I'm writing it to give you an idea of what my 15 minutes of fame were like, because even though I was technically a well-known college basketball player, as you'll soon see I had a completely different experience "in the spotlight" than your typical well-known college basketball player. As always, if you have a problem with me writing about this, you can go to your local supermarket, buy a couple of sticks of butter, glaze your forearm until it's nice and smooth, and hastily fist yourself.

A couple of months after Bob Baptist wrote about my blog in the *Columbus Dispatch*, I got an email from an AOL account claiming to be ESPN.com columnist Bill Simmons, asking if I'd be willing to do an interview for his podcast. Simmons had a following of millions and had been my favorite sportswriter for years, so I guess you could say that this was a pretty big deal. But instead of getting excited, I was certain the email was a hoax and deleted it. I didn't *think* it was a hoax. I *knew* it was a hoax, for a variety of reasons.

First of all, I knew that Simmons was widely considered to be the pioneer of sportswriting on the internet, so I assumed that he would be pretty internet-savvy. But this email came from an AOL account in 2008, which was a dead giveaway that whoever sent it was anything but "internet-savvy." Secondly, with the exception of Baptist writing a blurb about me on his blog, I hadn't gotten any media attention at any level. It seemed to me that the natural progression would've been for the Ohio State school paper to write about it, then maybe the *Dispatch*, then after that maybe a couple of papers from other Big Ten cities, until ultimately a couple of national outlets wrote something about it (if it ever got that far, of course). At the time, I had yet to do a single interview about my blog, so I wasn't buying for a second that my first interview was going to come from the most popular sports columnist on the planet instead of an Ohio State journalism student. Nothing about that made sense.

Lastly, my circle of friends knew that Simmons was pretty much the only sportswriter I regularly read, so I was certain that one of them had created a fake email account and was pretending to be Simmons because they thought that had the best chance of making me freak out from excitement. Had it been any other national sports columnist, I might have believed it, but this was like I started a garage band with my friends and we joked, "What if U2 wanted to collaborate with us?" before we even wrote a single song, and then Bono and The Edge showed up at my front door a couple of weeks later.

The day after I got the email, I called my buddy Keller, who has been my best friend since we both were in sixth grade, and told him that I didn't fall for his prank and it was a pretty awful attempt. He had no idea what I was talking about and assured me that he had nothing to do with the email. Although there was a chance he was just refusing to give up on his prank, I trusted him and sifted through my deleted mail to forward it to him per his request. After Keller read it, he told me he was 99 percent sure the email was real for a few reasons, most notably that he "remembered reading somewhere that Simmons had an AOL email address." I couldn't believe it.

It's embarrassing to admit now, but after my conversation with Keller I spent the entire day crafting a reply email to Simmons that was at least five paragraphs long. Even though all he was looking for was a simple, "Yeah, I'll come on your podcast" reply, I sent him an email that told him my life story and reeked of desperation, to which he responded by basically saying, "Cool story, bro." Also included in his response was a number for me to call the next day. With the possibility of it being a prank still lingering in my mind, I Googled the number and confirmed that it was in fact an ESPN number—and in doing so proved that the email most certainly was not a hoax.

The reality and magnitude of everything finally sank in. After doing a grand total of maybe three or four interviews in my entire career at Ohio State, I was now about to go on Bill Simmons's podcast. The next day I called the number I was given at the designated time and tried my hardest to mask my nervousness. The 10-minute interview felt like an eternity. In reality, it was more of a laid-back conversation than an interview, but the format was entirely irrelevant to me. The only thing I cared about was that my first legitimate interview was going to be heard by millions of people and the fact that it was for a podcast and not a print article meant that Simmons couldn't change my words around and make me sound cooler than I really was. No, the millions of people who were going to listen to this were going to hear my words straight from my mouth, which scared the absolute shit out of me.

After the interview ended, I hung up the phone, took a deep breath, and mentally braced myself for the inevitable outpouring of reaction. And what an outpouring it was. Just two days after I deleted Simmons's email and came so close to pissing away a great opportunity, my life was turned completely upside down and forever changed.

THIRTY-TWO

As I'm sure you can imagine, my blog exploded after I went on Simmons's podcast. After averaging around 1,000 page hits per day on the blog for its first few months (I thought that was a ton), the podcast appearance skyrocketed my page hits to 50,000 per day for at least a week, and even when the initial boom died down, I still maintained around 20,000 hits per day throughout the rest of the season, which was pretty mind-blowing. Of course, none of this really matters because anyone who measures the success of their blog based on their page hits is clearly doing it wrong.

Instead of counting page hits, blog success should be measured exclusively by the fans. And by that I mean that blog success should be measured by the amount of random encounters with fans and the unusual ways in which the fans choose to interact with you. You know, things like getting pet rabbits named after you or having a middle-aged man say, "I'll let you have my beautiful wife if you mention me on your blog," while his definitely-not-beautiful wife is standing right next to him. Yes, when you get a guy to offer you his wife in exchange for a simple shout-out and she is perfectly fine with it, you know that you've accomplished something.

The thing about my newfound "fame" was that I was far from being anything that could even remotely be interpreted as a celebrity and was instead just a guy that a few handfuls of people recognized. It's not like I was suddenly the big man on campus at Ohio State, which made the interactions with people who knew of me that much more fun. Had I been a full-fledged celebrity in Columbus like Jim Tressel or, to a lesser extent, The Villain and had to deal with people harassing me everywhere I went, I'm sure I would have hated it every time people stopped me in public to introduce themselves.

But because I was only noticed maybe once or twice every time I stepped outside of my apartment, fan interactions weren't overwhelming. It was kind of a nice stroke to my ego to finally get recognized after living in anonymity for my first two seasons with the team. Plus, the fan interactions were always so much fun for me (and still are) because it was always unpredictable as to who would be the one person that recognized me each time I was out in public. One time a guy sitting by me in one of my classes, who had been pretty reserved and shy for most of the semester, leaned over while our professor was talking and appeared as if he was going to ask me for a pen or a piece of paper (as if I ever brought pens or paper to class), but instead said, "Love the blog."

Another time I took my car to get some maintenance done, and a middle-aged car mechanic, who definitely did not fit into the target demographic for my blog, walked all the way over from the other side of the shop to tell me he was a fan. I even had elderly women and some of my professors recognize me. I truly did have a guerrilla fan base in the sense that they would seemingly disguise themselves among the rest of the general public and pop up out of nowhere to flatter me when I least expected it. And although I loved it every time it happened, no guerrilla interaction will ever top the time Erin Andrews surprised me at a restaurant in Champaign, Illinois.

By the time we played at Illinois in late January, I had already established a solid fan base, but I was far from being a household name in the world of college basketball. I liked this because I could write about people I spent a good deal of time around without having the things I wrote get back to them (because I knew there was no way in hell they were reading my blog).

I would frequently write on my blog about my plans to pull pranks on The Villain, sometimes even calling on my readers to assist me in pranking him, and for the longest time he would be oblivious to the source of the pranks even though I was publicly announcing what I was doing. Along the same lines, I would frequently write on my blog about my affection for Erin Andrews because I, like every other straight red-blooded American male, appreciated everything she brought to the world of sports, which is really just another way of saying I kinda wanted to put my face between her breasts (if you know what I mean).

Because Erin and I frequently crossed paths (she worked a lot of our games), and because when we did cross paths she would never have any reason to talk to me instead of my superstar teammates, I would write about my awkward interactions with her and play up the similarity between me and the stereotypical high school nerd who is afraid to talk to the cheer captain. I even went as far as pretending she and I were in a relationship on my blog, which further underscored the notion that I was a desperate loser and couldn't wait for the day when she'd finally acknowledge me. Well, when that day finally came, I couldn't have possibly been any more embarrassed.

Before we get to that, though, we have to first go back. Just before our home game against Indiana during my junior season, Erin walked over to our bench during our warm-up with a notebook in hand and sat down right in between Dave Lighty and me.

Dave and I both had foot injuries and were projected to be out for a while, but Erin obviously did not give a single shit about my injury because Dave was our leader and team captain and I was a worthless walk-on. When she sat down between the two of us, she turned her back to me to ask Dave how he was dealing with his injury, took down all the information she needed, and then stood up and walked away without so much as even acknowledging my presence. What's worse, during the game she actually pulled Dave aside for a live in-game interview, during which she failed to mention that he wasn't the only one on the team dealing with a serious foot injury.

Because this played out in front of our student section, and because my relationship with Erin had become one of the more prominent storylines on my blog, I knew this incident would be great fodder for a blog post. In the next few days, I wrote a post in which I called Erin out for turning her back to me. She had ignored me one too many times, and dammit, I just wasn't going to tolerate it anymore, so I had no choice but to publicly end my imaginary relationship with her. I was sure that this would send an effective message and she'd be devastated and come crawling back to me. And by that I mean that I was sure she had no idea I was writing about her so frequently and if she knew she'd probably think I was creepy as hell and get a restraining order against me.

Less than a week later, the entire team went to a Champaign restaurant the night before our game against Illinois. When we went to restaurants on the road like this, it wasn't unusual for the TV crew that was going to call the game to be there too, either by coincidence or because they wanted to pick Coach Matta's brain for information to use for their broadcast. Well, as we walked into this particular restaurant, it became clear not only that the TV crew was at the restaurant, but also that one of the members of the crew was none other than Erin Andrews herself.

As we all filed to the back of the restaurant, Coach Matta

waved at her while all of our managers freaked out and asked me if I had noticed that she was there. I told them that I had noticed, but that I didn't care because I was over her and had publicly ended our relationship, and then I went to my table and sat down with the rest of the team. And that was the end of that. Or so I thought.

About an hour later, a manager came up to me while I was eating my dinner and told me that he had just gone to the bathroom and, on his way back, Erin stopped him to ask specifically if I was in the restaurant with the team. I thought he was just trying to mess with me, so I told him to go fill up my water bottle and sit back down because I didn't believe him for a second. As he walked back to his table, though, Erin opened up the doors to our private dining room and stood still in the door frame as she scanned the room. I thought about what the manager had said, but I still assumed that she was looking for Coach Matta because she wanted to talk to him about the upcoming game or something. Just to be sure, I stopped eating and looked up from my dinner to see what her next move was going to be.

After a few beats, she finally opened her mouth and said, "Where's Titus? We need to talk!"

I was so stunned that I probably would have pissed myself had I not been fully erect.

She eventually found me and walked over to my table. "What's with all this talk about you breaking up with me?"

My face turned bright red, and as I tried to talk I ended up stuttering some gibberish instead. Once I calmed down and collected myself, I tried to explain to her that it was all a big joke and the only reason I ever started talking about our fake relationship was because I thought it would be funny to see if a walk-on benchwarmer could ever get her attention. But as it turned out, it was instead thoroughly embarrassing.

I continued pleading with her to believe that I wasn't as creepy as I seemed, and eventually she seemed satisfied with what I had to say, even though she had a "uh huh . . . suuuure" look on her face the entire time I was talking. This went on for the next five minutes or so until I asked her for her number, one thing led to another, yadda, yadda, yadda, I never really talked to her again. I'll let you fill in the details as you see fit.

THIRTY-THREE

Heading into my senior year at Ohio State, many people suggested that my blog had made me the most popular guy on our team, even though The Villain was a preseason All-American and projected to be a lottery pick in the NBA draft after the upcoming season. (He was eventually picked by the Philadelphia 76ers with the second overall pick in the 2010 draft.) This notion was, of course, completely wrong, but the fact that some people in the media suggested it seemed pretty incredible to me. After all, just two years earlier I was as big a nobody as you'll ever find in the world of college basketball, and now I was arguably the most popular player on a top ten team. To be anything more than an anonymous scrub on the end of the bench would have been a huge deal to me, so this attention was pretty mind-blowing.

By the time the end of November rolled around and we had already played a handful of games, The Villain had established himself as the front-runner to win the National Player of the Year Award (which he eventually did do), but the sports information director at Ohio State, who was in charge of organizing all of our interviews with the media, claimed that I was getting more interview requests than him. And honestly, it's hard to refute that claim. After going on Simmons's podcast, I kind of became the media darling on our team. Sportswriters all over the country thought I had a quirky and offbeat story that was unlike anything else in college basketball, so they seemed more interested in writing about The Shark and Club Trillion than writing another clichéd article about how good The Villain was. All of this attention didn't necessarily translate into more hits for my blog (not that I cared), but it certainly did translate into me getting recognized in public much more frequently.

It also led to me receiving unprecedented support from opposing teams' fans. Virtually everywhere we played, students from our rival schools would talk to me during our pregame warm-ups and tell me they were fans of my blog, tell me they appreciated what I was doing because they were benchwarmers in high school or something, or sometimes even ask me for an autograph (or all three).

This happened at literally every school in the Big Ten except Northwestern (probably because my lowbrow humor was too juvenile for their intellectual tastes) and Michigan (probably because it was too difficult for Michigan fans to read my blog and at the same time have Ohio State fans' balls slapping against their chins). Students from Wisconsin, Indiana, Purdue, and Iowa even made signs to show their support for Club Trillion. One sign at Indiana actually proposed marriage. A group of students from Minnesota took things another step further than that by starting a "We want Titus!" chant toward the end of our game with them my senior year. Yes, you read that right—Minnesota's student section actually started a chant at the end of a game for an opposing team's walk-on. I can't say for sure, but I think this might have been the first time something like this happened in the history of college basketball.

But as cool as it was to get a warm reception on the road, obviously nothing came close to how awesome the treatment from

Ohio State fans was. I've already mentioned how one middle-aged Ohio State fan asked for a shout-out in exchange for "his beautiful wife" and how one girl informed me that she had named her pet rabbit after me. What I haven't mentioned, though, is how I was asked to write a speech for a best man at a wedding because the groom was apparently a fan of mine, or how I was asked to throw out the first pitch at a community wiffleball tournament in the small town of Coldwater, Ohio. And I also haven't mentioned that sometime during my senior year I was offered a key to the city of Upper Sandusky, Ohio, which was something I particularly got a kick out of because Upper Sandusky was the hometown of my teammate Jon Diebler, and he told me that I was offered a key to his own hometown before he even was. (This is especially remarkable considering Upper Sandusky is a small town and Jon is treated like a god there.) I also got a kick out of it because the offer was eventually rescinded, but that kind of ruins the story, so let's just pretend that I actually was given a key to the city.

To go along with these random offers and encounters with fans, just about every home game during my senior season resulted in our student section belting out the "We want Titus!" chant toward the end of the game, even during games in which I was in street clothes because I was injured. I worked out a deal early in the season with the Ohio State compliance office that allowed me to sell T-shirts with my blog's logo on them so long as all the proceeds went to a charity, so every home game (and even some road games) featured throngs of fans wearing my shirts. In fact, my shirts became so popular among fans of my blog (otherwise known as the Trillion Man March) that by the time the season ended just a few months later thousands of shirts had been sold all over the world and over $50,000 had been raised for A Kid Again, which is a Columbus-based charity focused on enhancing the quality of life for kids with life-threatening illnesses. (Quick plug: if you live in Ohio, or anywhere for that matter, and are considering getting involved with a charity, make it this one. You won't find a better group of human beings than the people running A Kid Again, and interacting with the sick kids for five minutes will literally change your outlook on life.) There's no way to say this without sounding like a pompous asshole, so screw it, I'm not even going to try: I can't even begin to describe how humbling it was to raise $50,000 for A Kid Again despite being a walk-on benchwarmer who only scored nine career points. It is no doubt the single greatest accomplishment of my life, and there isn't even a close second.

The culmination of my 15 minutes of benchwarming fame came on my senior night against Illinois, which was the final home game of the year and would be the final home game of my career at Ohio State. The entire day leading up to the game, I had a camera crew from the Big Ten Network follow me around to film a documentary for their show *The Journey*, which only made the evening that much of a bigger deal for me. Also adding to the aura of the night was the fact that all of the 3,000 students in our student section were wearing my shirts and the fact that a win would clinch the regular season Big Ten title for us.

Not to give away any spoilers, but thanks largely to our student section wearing my shirts, chanting my name throughout the game, and just generally being the best student section in college basketball, I cried like a baby before and after the game and still get chills thinking about it. It was the most memorable night of my life, and I'm not saying that as hyperbole. I can vividly remember everything about that night and likely won't forget it as long as I live. When I think back on my four years at Ohio State, nothing else comes close to sticking out in my mind as much as my senior night. Not the National Championship from my freshman year. Not the numerous fights with The Villain. And not even Ivan's infamous beej.

I came to Ohio State as an unknown average kid who majored in math, aspired to be an orthopedic surgeon, and filled up water bottles for the basketball team as a hobby. And yet, on that senior night it was clear to me that I had somehow transformed into a local celebrity thanks to the combination of an absurd amount of luck and my inability to take anything seriously. I couldn't wrap my mind around it then and still can't wrap my mind around it now. All I know is that I was incredibly lucky to be in the position I was and will be forever indebted to Coach Matta, the media as a collective whole, and, most especially, the Ohio State fans. I may have only had 15 minutes in the spotlight, but I'll be damned if they weren't the most entertaining and exciting 15 minutes of my life.

(And with that, my autofellatio is officially over. Again, I apologize for seeming like a conceited asshole, but I promise my intention wasn't to brag about being "famous," mostly because I fully acknowledge that at best I was a quirky national story with a cult following and at worst I was just a guy a few people around Columbus knew. My intent was instead to give you, the reader, an inside look into my life in the [not really that bright] spotlight. I thought some of the things were bizarre and random and made for interesting stories, so if you didn't see it that way and instead interpreted it as me blowing my own horn, I'm sorry. As always, if you really have that big of a problem, I'm perfectly fine with letting you lick my chode.

Now, let's get back to the good stuff.)

PART SEVEN

*All you'll ever be is a couch potato bum who mooches
and rides coattails.*

—The Villain

THIRTY-FOUR

We opened up the 2009–2010 season with a 40-point win over Alcorn State (thanks in large part to The Villain's first career triple-double) and another blowout win over James Madison to advance to the semifinals of the 2K Sports Classic, where we were to play defending national champion and fourth-ranked North Carolina in our first big game of the season. The Tar Heels jumped out to a big lead on us right from the tip and maintained a double-digit lead for most of the game until we mounted a furious comeback and carved the deficit down to two before the final buzzer. We ran out of time with our comeback attempt and came up a little bit short, losing by just four in a game that all along seemed like we were about to get blown out of. In other words, it was what we in the business refer to as a relatively good loss, even though the term "good loss" seems like it's as big of an oxymoron as a hooker named Chastity.

The North Carolina loss set up a consolation game matchup against 12th-ranked Cal, which was a game that was a bit of role reversal in that this time we were the ones who jumped out to a huge lead and eventually let Cal claw their way back into the game. But like our comeback attempt against North Carolina, Cal ultimately ran out of time and we won by six, giving us our first marquee win of the young season.

In our next game, we beat Lipscomb pretty easily on the back of The Villain's second triple-double in five games (well, third if you count his 23-point, 11-rebound, and 10-turnover performance against North Carolina). Coming into the season, there had only ever been one triple-double in Ohio State history (Dennis Hopson in 1987), so for The Villain to have two in only our first five games was quite an accomplishment. It was still early, and there was a lot of basketball left to be played, but through the season's first few weeks The Villain had already established himself as the front-runner to win the National Player of the Year Award and was seriously flirting with obliterating the Ohio State record book.

The Lipscomb win was followed up with an absolute curb-stomping of St. Francis (Pennsylvania) in which we won by 63 and destroyed them so badly that I got to play a career-high five minutes. I also recorded another career high in that game with two shot attempts in those five minutes, but since I missed them both and in the process embarrassed myself and shamed my family, I don't really want to talk about it. Let's just move on.

After the St. Francis win, we beat a pretty good Florida State team at home in the ACC–Big Ten Challenge and in the process helped the Big Ten clinch a collective victory over the ACC for the first time in the 11-year history of the event. Following that, we beat Eastern Michigan by 51 to set up a top-20 matchup at Butler with our next game. But even though the box score from the Eastern Michigan win might make it seem like the game was business as usual, it was actually far from it.

That's because, with about 12 minutes left in the first half, The Villain drove to the basket and was nudged from behind by an Eastern Michigan player as he went up for the dunk, which threw off his balance ever so slightly and caused him to lose his grip on the rim as his body swung toward the baseline. His momentum continued to carry his feet upward until he lost his grip on the rim and let go, resulting in him plummeting to the floor and landing square on his lower back with a loud thud, kinda like how Antoine Tyler fell in *The 6th Man*. And with that, the best player in college basketball and the one guy we absolutely could not afford to lose had a broken back and was out not only for the rest of the Eastern Michigan game, but also for the foreseeable future.

It goes without saying, but I'll say it anyway: this was not good. In fact, one could argue that because he was the best player in college basketball and was directly responsible for most of our team's success, his injury was detrimental to us because it appeared as though we weren't going to achieve the same amount of success we would have otherwise achieved had he not broken his back.

Simply put, our team's collective mood when Evan went down could best be summarized by the immortal dying words of Gen. George Armstrong Custer at the Battle of the Little Bighorn:

"Oh, shit."

THIRTY-FIVE

T he first game on the schedule following The Villain's back injury was against 20th-ranked Butler on the road. To add insult to The Villain's injury, I often acknowledged him as either "cheesedick" or "twat lips." And to add an unfavorable situation for our team to The Villain's injury, Butler was really good that year and actually played in the National Championship game at the end of the season where, according to John Brenkus of Sport Science, they were only 0.5 miles per hour and 3 inches away from winning the thing. It would have been tough to beat them at their place with The Villain, so I figured we were screwed now that we were playing for the first time without a guy who literally had the ball in his hands during offensive possessions more than every other guy on the team combined. And as is usually the case with most things, I was absolutely right: we lost to Butler by eight.

After the Butler loss, we blew out Presbyterian by 30, beat Delaware State by 16, and took care of business against a decent

Cleveland State team at home to head into the Christmas break on a three-game winning streak. We hadn't exactly rattled off three marquee wins or anything, but it was a three-game winning streak nonetheless, and it was encouraging to see us have some measure of success without The Villain. Since we were on a winning streak and there were good vibes in our locker room, and since we had over a week off in between our games because of Christmas break, I decided it was a perfect time to play a prank on one of our coaches. I targeted Coach Jeff Boals, who had joined the coaching staff from Akron right after my junior season ended, because he was undoubtedly my favorite coach. Even though I had only known him for eight months at the time, I had already gotten a good read on him and was pretty confident he would appreciate a good prank, so I asked Keller to help me come up with something.

Keller and I are both notoriously lazy, so we wanted something that would require minimal effort on our part. Ultimately, we decided to create a fake email account and send Boals a hateful email. We created a character that was supposed to be a stereotypical redneck from rural Ohio, which is another way of saying we created a character who was an uneducated racist homophobe, had tons of pent-up anger, and loved his Buckeyes probably a little too much. Since Keller is a master at writing as if he's someone else, I let him write the bulk of the email, and I contributed basically by just giving him a handful of ideas and providing details about Coach Boals to make the email more personal.

(Please keep in mind as you read it that we were playing a character and chose to make our character racist and homophobic only because we wanted him to come across as hateful, which we thought would make the prank more effective since it would give the email a threatening tone. If, for whatever reason, you do get offended, you'll have to take your complaint to Keller, since he's the one who wrote it. But if you aren't offended and think it's funny, give me credit since I'm the one who wrote it.)

Listen here, you four-eyed fuck.

I made the mistake of going to an Ohio State basketball game and the program that my fucking girlfriend
made me buy had some glasses wearing doofus on the
front cover. After discovering that this liberal fucking
state doesn't sell beer at the games, I took to reading the
program. Lo and behold, the loser I saw on the front
turned out to be you, Mr. Bowls. Could there be a bigger
fucking pansy on this planet than you? Honestly, you
were wearing a pink shirt. Unless you have breast cancer,
stop wearing such faggy colors. The last time I checked,
my Buckeyes' colors were Scarlet and Gray, not Scarlet
and Gay. It's complete horseshit that the legacy of this
fine university is being tarnished by some nearsighted
poopdick.

A bigger fucking travesty than the decision to hire
some jizz fiend who walks on the treadmill so his sweat
doesn't mess up his gelled hair is to leave #34 on the
bench. That guy is on fucking fire every single time in
warm-ups. I honestly watched that badass make 3-pointer
after 3-pointer only to be banished to the bench because
douchetards like you feel threatened by his ability. Just
cause you and your bum ACL can't check the man with
the hot hand doesn't mean you should keep him on the
bench when he could be lighting up the arena for 50+ a
night, you jealous dick. Seriously, if you can't get on board
with #34 getting buckets all over random black kids, then
I question your love for America. And to think, every time
he doesn't get to go nothing but net from 25 feet away,
you're taking away an opportunity for the girls in the
crowd to get their titties hard about the guy. So you're not
only a douche, but a cockblocking homo as well.

In conclusion, you should be fucking fired, and that
Mark Titus guy is the key to the Buckeyes winning the
title. Take the dong out of your mouth, and put that fuck-

ing guy in the game, or you'll be sorry. I figured a gay
nerd with glasses as thick as yours would be able to see
talent when that's close in front of your face. Guess not,
you fucking moron.

Best regards,
Dale R. "Woody" Thornton III

Because Dale "Woody" Thornton kept making references to
playing me more, we were sure that Boals would figure out that
I was behind the prank. But somehow he didn't make the con-
nection. At practice the next day he approached me and asked if I
knew some guy named Dale, which prompted me to laugh and ask
him if he enjoyed the email. Confusion spread across his face as if
he was trying to figure out how I knew about the email, leading me
to believe that he was trying to counter-prank me. I reluctantly bit
on the bait and explained that I was responsible for the email, and
his face lit up.

"You son of a bitch," he said. "I thought some redneck wanted
to kill me."

I still wasn't buying that he didn't know I was behind the email.
He insisted that he didn't and even offered proof. "You can even go
talk to Debbie [the secretary in the basketball office who is by all
accounts a nice, wholesome lady]. All of the coaches' emails go to
her first, and she forwards us the ones she thinks we need to read.
She told me I got some hate mail, so I asked her to send it to me.
We both read it and thought it was hilarious, but we were sure it
was real."

After he told me this, I was initially pumped that my prank had
worked, but I quickly changed my feeling when I realized what
exactly he had said. The fact that Debbie was the first to read the
email probably makes the story funnier and better, so I'm cool with
it now, but in that moment I couldn't have been more embarrassed.
I darted up to her office, apologized a thousand times, told her I
honestly didn't think anybody but Boals would read it, and tried to
explain to her that she was just collateral damage. She seemed to

accept my apology, but the tone in her voice and her body language told me that she did so only so I would leave her office and just stop talking about it altogether. Whoops.

Perhaps Boals should have taken Dale's advice and found a way to play me more in our next game at Wisconsin, because the substitution pattern we did use certainly didn't work. After the first eight minutes of the game went back and forth, the Buzzcuts jumped out to a big lead to close the first half and never looked back, as they ended up beating us by 22, which was our worst loss of the season. Since it was my last trip to Madison, the loss meant that the Kohl Center was the only Big Ten arena that I never won in, which was especially upsetting since I knew we would have most likely won had The Villain been healthy.

Nonetheless, we had a chance to bounce back from the Wisconsin loss by playing at Michigan a few days later. But not having The Villain proved to be costly yet again, as Michigan used a late run to beat us by nine. Again, it was frustrating to know that we probably would have also beat Michigan had The Villain been healthy, but it was even more frustrating to know that since The Villain hurt his back against Eastern Michigan, whose campus is just 15 minutes away from Michigan's campus, and since we played Michigan just a couple weeks after Eastern Michigan, I was pretty confident that Michigan had asked Eastern Michigan to do them a favor and take out The Villain because they're a bunch of cheating asshole bastards.

But that's just my theory. Whether I'm right or wrong, at the end of the day we were 0–2 in the Big Ten and had lost half of our last six games. We needed either to figure out how to play without The Villain or to cross our fingers and hope he made a miraculous recovery and saved our season before it was too late.

THIRTY-SIX

Despite being told that he'd be out for at least eight weeks, The Villain made a miraculous recovery and saved our season before it was too late after just four and a half weeks. In his first game back, he started and played just half the game against Indiana at home, and while he only scored eight points and pulled down just four rebounds, we didn't really need much from him because Indiana sucked donkey balls.

After we blew the Hoosiers out by 25, we went on the road and lost to a relatively good Minnesota team by nine. Against Indiana, our chemistry imbalance wasn't a huge deal because Indiana was awful, but our inability to get The Villain fully integrated back into the team proved much more costly against a good team like Minnesota. Whatever the case, we dropped to just 1–3 in the Big Ten, which was good enough for eighth place in the conference. After having our sights set on winning the Big Ten title at the start of the season, four games into conference play it seemed as if we'd be lucky to even finish in the top half of the standings.

Shortly after the Minnesota game, I was approached by the

Ohio State SID, who told me that a reporter with OSU's student newspaper, *The Lantern*, wanted to talk to me for an article he was writing about the basketball managers. Since Danny and I both started our careers at Ohio State as managers, he wanted to ask us how our role on the team had changed and what our relationship was like with the current managers. I told him that I'd be willing to do the interview, mostly because I'm a media whore and I'm always flattered when people want to interview me, but Danny said he didn't want to talk to the reporter.

That's because ever since Danny walked-on, he did whatever he could to distance himself from his past as a manager. (He had been a manager for a full year before he walked-on.) For whatever reason, it was a point of pride for him that he had a jersey to wear during the games (rightfully so) and was therefore—in his mind—a real part of the team now, so he didn't like revisiting the fact that he used to be a manager and would actually get offended when people reminded him of his managerial past. So, naturally, I would use the fact that he got upset so easily against him whenever the opportunity would arise. Such as now.

I called the number our SID gave me and talked to the reporter for about five minutes. When the interview was over, the reporter said, "Thanks for taking time to do this, but can I ask one more favor? Is there any way you can get me Danny Peters's number? I'm trying to talk to him for this article, but I'm having a hard time getting a hold of him."

To buy myself time to figure out how I wanted to attack this, I told the guy that I would absolutely give him Danny's number, but that since it was in my phone I'd have to hang up on him and just text him the number in a few minutes. He said he was cool with that, so we both hung up, and I racked my brain for a couple of minutes before it hit me that I really only had one option.

I quickly called Keller and as soon as he answered the phone, I said, "Keller! Do you want to be Danny?"

He responded, "Of course I don't."

"I don't mean it as a hypothetical question. Listen, a reporter from *The Lantern* just interviewed me and said he wants to interview Danny too, but Danny has made it clear that he doesn't want to do the interview. I told the *Lantern* guy that I'd give him Danny's number, but I'm thinking I should give him your number and you should act like Danny when he calls."

This was a game-changer for Keller. "I'm in."

I explained to him that in order for the prank to really work, he should say things that were the complete opposite of what Danny would say, so he should talk about how much he loved being a manager (specifically doing the bitch work), he should talk about how he took the current managers out for milkshakes and french fries all the time, and he should just generally be as douchey as he possibly could. He told me he'd take care of it, so I hung up on him, texted the *Lantern* guy Keller's number, and waited.

An hour later, Keller called me to tell me he had done the interview, and he could hardly hold in his laughter. He went on to tell me that during the interview he had found a way to say all of the following things as if he was Danny:

"The best part about being a manager was getting to fill up water bottles and wipe sweat off the floor. All the other managers hated doing that, but I loved it because I knew I was making a difference."

"I know what it takes to be a manager at such a high level, so to show my appreciation for our managers, I invite them over for a sleepover at my place at least once a month. It's a good opportunity for us to bond, and I think they really have a lot of fun."

"I like being a player, but I think I'll like it more when my dream comes true and I finally dribble down the court, pass to my best friend Mark Titus, and watch him sink a three-pointer while the crowd chants his name. That would just be awesome."

"Yeah, Mark and I have been best buds for a while. We actually have a nickname for ourselves—Los Dos Amigos. It's like we're the Three Amigos, except there's only two of us."

A couple of days later, the article ran, and while it quoted Danny only once, it was enough to grab his attention. (The quote they used basically just had Danny saying that "playing on this team is a dream come true.") He somehow found out that he had been quoted in the article and when he did, he immediately knew that I was behind it. Later that day, when we were back at our apartment, I told Danny that it could have been a lot worse and shared with him some of Keller's gems. This seemed to upset him more, but he also realized that he pretty much had no choice but to just laugh at this point.

A few weeks later, once Danny thought this incident had blown over, I shared the story with a couple of guys in our student section before one of our home games. They thought it was hilarious, and when our next home game rolled around they told me they had a surprise in store. When that particular game was in its waning moments and we had a big lead, I made eye contact with the guys in the student section and raised my eyebrows, as if to say, *Where is this surprise?*

They each gave me a head nod, reached underneath their seats, pulled out sombreros, ponchos, and fake mustaches, and proceeded to chant "Los Dos Amigos! Los Dos Amigos!" until Danny and I checked in. (They continued this routine for the rest of the season.) I absolutely lost it on the bench as I pointed them out to Danny. Nobody else in the crowd and nobody else on our team had any idea what the costumes or chants were for, but that didn't matter. Danny knew, and there's no doubt in my mind that deep down it bugged him at least a little bit. And that's really what's important.

Following our loss at Minnesota, we went on the road to play sixth-ranked Purdue at their place. Purdue was the cream of the Big Ten crop at that point in the season while, as previously mentioned, we were just 1–3 in conference play going into this game. It felt like this was the biggest game of the year since an upset would put us back on track and do wonders for our confidence, and a blowout loss (which was entirely plausible) would all but eliminate any chance we had at winning the Big Ten title.

In the first half, Purdue played just like they were the best team in the conference, and one of the best in the country, as they rode the back of Robbie Hummel's 29 first-half points and torched our zone defense en route to a 12-point halftime lead. But in the second half, we switched out of our zone and went with the more conventional man-to-man defense, which initially didn't make much difference because they held on to a double-digit lead throughout most of the second half. But with 7:30 left in the game and a 13-point deficit staring us in the face, we finally decided to play with a sense of urgency, which quickly proved to be what we had been missing all along.

On offense we decided to just give the ball to The Villain and get the hell out of the way, which was something we also should have probably done sooner, because he absolutely exploded and singlehandedly got us back in it when he scored every point during a 10–0 run that tied the game with 2:30 remaining. When Purdue called time-out, Coach Matta gave his "Their assholes are tight!" speech again, only this time he was absolutely right—Purdue's assholes were most certainly tight. We made a few clutch plays in the game's waning moments, and Purdue let a few opportunities slip away, and when the final buzzer sounded, the scoreboard showed a four-point advantage in our favor.

This was a monumental win for us because, less than a week after The Villain returned from a serious injury, we beat the sixth-ranked team in the country and perennial favorite to win the Big Ten title on their home court, which restored our confidence and revived our season. We had finally fully integrated The Villain back into the rotation, and we were now ready to make the rest of the Big Ten our collective bitch. Nothing was going to stand in our way. Well, nothing except another integral player on our team going down with a career-ending injury.

THIRTY-SEVEN

I originally hurt my left shoulder sometime around Thanksgiving, when Dallas did a swim move to get around me as I was fronting him in the post and he dropped his elbow on my shoulder and made it pop. (Yes, Dallas was responsible for both the foot injury during my junior year that forced me to sit out for 12 weeks and the shoulder injury during my senior year that ended my career.) Being the warrior that I am, I toughed it out for a couple of months and continued practicing and playing through the pain. As the calendar turned to January and approached February, though, the pain became greater and I had no choice but to approach Coach Matta in his office and ask him to reduce my playing time, which was a request that he responded to by laughing and saying, "Get the hell out of my office. I've got work to do."

As my shoulder became more and more painful, we had more and more success. We got The Villain back into the lineup and bounced back from a bad start in the Big Ten season by beating Purdue at their place, getting revenge on the 16th-ranked Buzzcuts at home, and dismantling Northwestern shortly thereafter. This combination of pain in my shoulder and success for the team resulted in me having virtually no responsibilities during our practices whatsoever. That's because when we started playing better, our practices became shorter, which resulted in my teammates needing me to sub in for them far less often (and by that I mean pretty much not at all). Even when they would think that they needed a sub, they would remember that I had a bum shoulder and would graciously change their mind as they suddenly realized that they weren't as tired as they originally thought.

Since I was essentially serving no purpose at all during our practices, with each passing day my feeling of invisibility on the team increased. Every now and then I would leave practice for a half-hour to take a dump and come back to find that nobody knew that I was even gone. Eventually it got to the point that every single day before practice I would hide my phone in a nearby bathroom so I could play Angry Birds or get on the internet while I took my mid-practice poop. I also made sure that these mid-practice poops would always take place right as soon as Coach Matta announced that it was time for defensive drills.

You know how girls who spend a lot of time together somehow have their periods synch up to happen at the exact same time? Well, similarly, my body somehow synched up to our practice schedule so that I had to take mammoth dumps whenever it was time for us to practice defense. And by "my body somehow synched up" what I really mean is that I acted like I had to poop and excused myself from practice, went to the bathroom and sat on the toilet, and screwed around on my phone for a half-hour without so much as squeezing out a single turd.

After a few weeks of this, I decided to go for what I thought would be the mother lode of all "see if they notice I'm gone" stunts. Despite what the wording in that last sentence might have led you to believe, I wasn't planning on committing suicide and I wasn't planning on fleeing the country unannounced, but I was instead planning to see if I could sit in the press box at the top of our arena and watch one of our practices.

On a day that wasn't particularly different from any other, I put on my practice gear and went onto our main floor to warm up just like I did every other day for practice. Once our warm-up was complete and our pre-practice shooting drills were done, I continued my daily routine and walked over to the sideline of the court and sat on the scorer's table while the real players did whatever it was they did on the court. After about five minutes of catching my breath, I decided to make my move.

I walked down the sideline toward the end of the court where the rest of the team was practicing, turned at the baseline, walked right in front of Coach Matta and an assistant coach, and pointed myself toward the tunnel that would take me to the elevator. As soon as I stepped off the temporary wooden court that had been laid down in the arena and stepped onto the permanent concrete, I felt a rush of anxiety come over me as I thought for sure someone would notice me and ask where I was going, especially since the restrooms were the complete opposite direction and there was no reason why I should have been walking toward that particular tunnel.

But then I remembered that I was nonexistent during practice and assured myself that nobody would even know I was gone. Once I made it to the elevator, I breathed a sigh of relief, rode the thing to the top of the arena, and sat in the press box high above the court on which our ongoing practice was taking place. When practice was about to end about an hour later, I rode the elevator back down and walked confidently back to my spot by the scorer's table with the kind of strut that only a guy who regularly thinks to himself, *Yeah, I run shit,* would walk with. Five minutes later, Coach Matta announced that the practice was over and asked everyone to "bring it in." And with that, I completed the easiest and single most relaxing basketball practice of my life.

After the practice, I joined the guys in the locker room and asked if anyone knew that I was gone. Obviously none of them had noticed (other than Danny, whom I had told I was going up to the press box right as I started walking toward the elevator), so I asked the same question of the managers, and they all had the same response. Determined to see if I really did go entirely unnoticed, I found Coach Boals by the coaches' locker room and asked him if any of the coaches had noticed I had left practice and sat up in the press box for pretty much the entirety of the practice. He told me that none of the coaches would notice if I got butt naked and started doing cartwheels on the sideline during practice, so of course they didn't notice that I left. Touché.

A few days later, I mentioned to Coach Matta during a team meal what I had done, and he just laughed and said, "That doesn't surprise me." Not that I needed it, but right then and there it was confirmed that I could in fact get away with anything I wanted both on and off the basketball court. I'm pretty sure every other coach in the country would've kicked my ass off the team within seconds of finding out about my shenanigans (and Bob Knight would've probably castrated me), yet Coach Matta thought it was funny.

A couple days after my press box incident, I woke up to go to class (perhaps this was my big mistake) and could barely move my left shoulder. I hadn't necessarily reinjured it, but I had tweaked it a few times since the original injury, and it seemed as though all those tweaks had finally caught up to me. When I told Vince that I could barely move my shoulder, he made me go get an MRI with our team doctor, who looked over the results and informed me that I had torn my labrum. Vince had originally diagnosed my injury as that very thing months before just from using his super athletic trainer intuition, but we had decided to just do some rehab and hope the shoulder improved on its own since we assumed it wasn't that bad of a tear.

But the MRI showed that it actually was a significant tear and wasn't going to improve on its own anytime soon, meaning surgery was all but inevitable. Our doctor informed me that a labrum repair surgery would put me out for at least six months. Since it was the tail end of January at the time, this meant I wouldn't be able to even start rehabbing my shoulder until July, which would've been four months after our season and my career ended.

As the doctor broke this news to me, my eyes welled up with tears from the combination of pain in my shoulder and knowing that my career had abruptly ended. Overcome with the emotion of the moment, I looked him in the eye and said, "Doc, I ain't going out like no bitch."

He responded, "I don't understand what you're saying," so I explained to him that I wanted to postpone the surgery so I could put on the Ohio State jersey one last time for my senior night. He said he was cool with that idea, but warned me that there was no way I could practice or play until then, so I would have to wear street clothes on the bench for the rest of the season. Bummer.

And so it was settled—except for the one encore appearance for my senior night, my career at Ohio State, and thus my basketball career in its entirety, was over. Although, to be fair, since I was a walk-on, it was debatable as to whether my career ever actually started in the first place.

THIRTY-EIGHT

We went on the road for my first game in street clothes and took on 12th-ranked West Virginia right in the heart of where incest, coonskin caps, and John Denver songs run rampant. We came into the game ranked just 25th, but we were playing our best basketball of the season at the time and were realistically much better than the 25th-best team in America. This seemed especially true when we jumped out to a big lead in the first half and led by 12 at halftime. But the second half was a different story: West Virginia opened up with a 10–0 run before ultimately taking the lead and never looking back.

We bounced back from that six-point loss a couple of days later and took care of Iowa with an eight-point win. As I'm sure you remember, our previous trip to Iowa resulted in me spending at least a half-hour on the toilet immediately after the game and making the entire team wait on the bus for me because I had suppressed my diarrhea for so long. Well, this time around I was thrilled to not have to deal with that again.

And by "not have to deal with that again" all I really mean is that I didn't make the team wait on me. I still had the overwhelm-ing feeling that I was about to shit my pants toward the end of the game, I still had to rush through the handshake line after the game so I could get to the toilet as soon as possible, and I still missed Coach Matta's entire postgame speech because I was sitting on the toilet as I pooped out what felt like scalding hot razor blades.

Two years in a row of this happening makes me believe that either Iowa was trying to poison me or the hotel we stayed at had some pretty terrible food. Either way, it goes without saying that I couldn't possibly be more proud about my streak of having diar-rhea every time I go to Iowa's campus. And just so we're clear, I've yet to return to Iowa City since this second incident, so technically the streak is still intact.

The Iowa win started a six-game win streak for us (the longest of the season up to that point) as we beat Minnesota, Penn State, Iowa again, Indiana, and Illinois shortly thereafter, extending our record to 20–6. More importantly than our overall record was the fact that we were now 10–3 in the Big Ten—good enough to share the top spot in the conference standings—after opening the con-ference season with just a 1–3 record. But while it may seem like we miraculously clawed our way back into the thick of the Big Ten race, the reality was that we only beat teams in the Big Ten that were considered either average or absolutely terrible. Up next was the real test. We had back-to-back games with Purdue and Michi-gan State, who were the two teams that we shared the conference lead with.

The good news heading into the Purdue game was that it was at home, where we hadn't lost a game all season and had really been pretty dominant considering we won every home game by double digits except for one (beat the Buzzcuts by just nine). But the bad news was that Purdue was ranked fourth in the country and had been playing out of their minds ever since we beat them at their place earlier in the year. They came out on fire for our rematch game and, in the words of Coach Matta, "shot the piss out of the ball" (60 percent from the field) en route to a 13-point halftime lead.

And while we eventually cut the lead to two with less than 10 minutes to play in the second half, we could never get over the hump and lost by three in a game that we never led.

That loss was devastating because it knocked us out of first place, but making things even worse was the fact that we had to turn around and travel to East Lansing to play 11th-ranked Michigan State in our very next game. We had historically always played the Spartans pretty well, so I was relatively confident heading into the game, even though we were playing a highly ranked team on the road. My confidence was affirmed when we went on a 15–0 run midway through the first half and took a 12-point lead into halftime.

But my confidence also quickly shattered when Michigan State came storming back in the second half and played like they really did belong on the top of the Big Ten standings. (They were still in a tie with Purdue for first place at this point.) The Spartans took the lead with four minutes left, but we finished on a 13–5 run and won by seven. This meant we were back in contention for the Big Ten title, but since we had one more loss than Purdue and didn't have any more games with them, we still needed another team to help us out and knock off the Boilers.

We got the help we needed from two different teams. On our way back to Columbus after we beat Penn State in our next game, word spread throughout the plane that Purdue's Robbie Hummel had torn his ACL during Purdue's game with Minnesota that was yet to finish. This was huge news, not only because Hummel was arguably Purdue's best player and their game with Minnesota still hung in the balance, but also because they still had to play Michigan State one last time, which would have been a tough game for them even with Hummel. Somehow Purdue squeaked out a win at Minnesota, but with a huge game between Purdue and Michigan State looming large, we knew there was still a chance for us to get at least a share of the Big Ten title. All we had to do was take care of business in our last two games and hope that Michigan State came through for us against Purdue.

The first opponent standing in our way was Michigan, who had as good of a chance at stopping us as you would have at stopping a pride of hungry lions by using nothing but a slinky. Translation: we were Ohio State and they were Michigan, so naturally we had our way with them and punched them square in their vaginas right from the start.

A fun story about this game with Michigan is that about an hour and a half before tipoff I took the elevator back up to the press box at the top of the arena, only this time I brought a couple of basketballs with me. While I was up in the press box during practice, I noticed that there was a door that led to the network of catwalks directly above the court, so obviously I wanted to try to shoot a ball from the catwalks to the basket 120 feet below. I rode the elevator to the top, walked through the door to the catwalks like I owned the building, and maneuvered my way around until I was as close as I could get to standing directly over the basket, which really wasn't even that close. (I stood directly above a spot that was probably about 20 feet away from the sideline of the court.)

Since fans had already started filing into the arena, I knew that I'd have to move quickly. I lined up the first shot as best I could and let it fly. Now, I didn't make it and honestly didn't even come close, but what I did do was cause one of the guys working on the catwalks to flip his shit. Right after the first ball hit the ground, I heard a voice yell, "Titus! No! No! Get the fuck down from here! Get the fuck down right now!"

With the guy screaming at the top of his lungs, I said, "My bad," chucked the second ball, and took off running. What this has to do with the game, I'm not sure, but I do know that I pissed off one of the workers at our arena, and more importantly, I do know that one of the workers at the arena knows my name. And that's almost better than hitting a shot from the catwalks. Almost.

The day after our game with Michigan, Purdue squared off with Michigan State and looked like a team in complete disarray without Hummel (and rightfully so). Purdue brought the intensity they needed and defended pretty well, but without Hummel's offensive skills, they could only muster 44 points and lost to Michigan State by nine. Suddenly, our last game of the year against Illinois turned into a Big Ten championship clincher for us, which would've been a big deal by itself, but it was an even bigger deal for me since it was my senior night and, since I was scheduled to have surgery on my shoulder the next day, it was going to be the last time I ever wore an Ohio State jersey.

As I mentioned earlier, the night felt like my own personal Super Bowl, given everything at stake and the fact that the Big Ten Network followed me around all day for a documentary. When I got to the arena and went out to the court to warm up, I was greeted by the sight of 3,000 students wearing shirts with my blog's logo on them and hitting a bunch of inflatable sharks in the air like beach balls, which only added even more to the already special night. But more remarkable than all of that was the fact that The Villain wore one of my shirts during our warm-up that actually had "The Villain" screen-printed on the back of it.

People often ask me what kind of relationship The Villain and I actually had and if we legitimately disliked each other or if I exaggerated our disdain for one another just to make my blog more interesting. I think him wearing my shirt on my senior night (and what would be his last home game at Ohio State because he went pro at the end of that season) kind of answers that question. The truth is that we really did fight like cats and dogs, and the truth is that we legitimately did dislike one another for extended periods of time during our careers as teammates, so I didn't exactly exaggerate *everything* I wrote on my blog.

But the truth is also that he and I fully respect one another and more often than not get along. Really, we were like brothers who fight like crazy but deep down care for one another, wish each other well in life, and support each other, which was evident when he wore my shirt on senior night. Also, just about every day, either before or after practice, he would honestly get butt naked except for his shoes and practice his ballhandling in front of a mirror while his dick swung back and forth and the rest of us on the team covered our eyes in disgust. What does that have to do with my relationship with The Villain, you ask? Well, to be honest, it really doesn't have anything to do with it. I just felt like telling an unflattering story about him to embarrass him because he's an ass-munch who needs to be knocked down a peg or two. Seriously, screw that guy.

The combination of the magnitude of the moment and the senior night festivities made me bawl my eyes out before the game even started. I ended up catching a lot of flak from people for this, but looking back on that night I honestly don't know how I could have not cried. As I stood out at midcourt, I was overcome with unadulterated emotion from seeing all the shirts in the student section and hearing everyone chanting my name when I got introduced. Ever since I was four years old, I had dreamed about that very moment, and now it was a reality. And so I cried like I had never cried before. It was inevitable.

As for the actual game, we let Illinois hang around a little more than we probably would've liked, but then pulled away with about 10 minutes left and took a 13-point lead into the game's final five minutes. With us firmly holding on to that 13-point lead as the clock ticked down to under two minutes, the student section burst into a "We want Titus!" chant that reverberated throughout the arena and still gives me chills to think about. After a minute of chanting, our lead extended to 16 and Coach Matta looked down to the end of the bench and gave me the nod.

Even though it was pretty painful to move my shoulder at all at that point, I let adrenaline take over and essentially just stood in the corner as I made the final trillion of my career a perfect game by not even touching the ball (while also recording a plus-minus of 0). When the final buzzer sounded, our student section flooded onto the court, and a handful of fans picked me up, put me on their shoulders, and paraded me around the court as we celebrated our Big Ten championship. I distinctly remember thinking to myself that my life would never get better than that moment right there, which kinda makes it equal parts memorable and depressing.

But since I consider myself to be a bit of an optimist, I like to focus more on the memorable aspect of that night and recall this fact: the last time I ever wore an Ohio State jersey, we won the Big Ten championship on my senior night and I recorded a perfect game trillion as thousands of people waved inflatable sharks in the air and chanted my name before storming the court and parading me around on a couple of fans' shoulders.

With the exception of maybe adding some explosions and boobs, I don't think it could've possibly been scripted any better.

THIRTY-NINE

T hanks to a strong end to the regular season and a little help from Minnesota (who I'm giving credit for indirectly making Hummel tear his ACL) and Michigan State, we were given the number-one seed in the Big Ten Tournament via a series of tiebreakers with Purdue and Michigan State. With this number-one seed, we received a bye into the tournament's second round, where we played Michigan for the second time in as many weeks after the Wolverines beat Iowa in the first round. Michigan entered the game with a 15–16 record, which meant they needed two more wins in the Big Ten Tournament to even be eligible for the NIT, and it also meant that a loss to us would end their season. Knowing this, Michigan played with a sense of urgency the entire game, whereas we just went through the motions. But even so, we were able to close the first half on a bit of a run and take a nine-point lead into the halftime break.

When the second half started, we picked up where we left off and extended our lead to 12 early on, but Michigan came storming back to cut the lead to just four. We responded with a 9–0 run to push the lead back up to 13 with a little over 10 minutes left and seemed to be on the brink of blowing them out. But yet again, they were too desperate for a win to just go away, and they chipped into our lead until they tied the game when Stu Douglass hit a three with 1:06 left on the clock. The Villain missed a layup on our next possession, and Michigan's Manny Harris hit a jumper to give them the lead with 30 seconds left. We opted to try to score quickly instead of holding the ball for one last shot, and Lighty hit a runner in the lane to tie the game with 14 seconds left, prompting Michigan to call time-out to set up a final play.

Once both teams broke their time-out huddles, Michigan took the ball out at half-court and inbounded it to Manny Harris, their best player and one of the best players in the Big Ten that year. He took a couple of dribbles to run off a little bit of clock, then came off a ball screen going to his right, pulled up just inside the elbow, and let the fadeaway shot fly.

Swish.

Damn.

There were still three seconds left on the clock, so we called time-out to set up a desperation play, which ended up being "get the ball to The Villain and hope he saves us." Since we had to take the ball out under Michigan's basket and go the full length of the floor, the plan was to get The Villain the ball as he was on the run, have him get as far as he possibly could in three seconds, and then let the shot fly and hope for the best.

We broke the time-out huddle, and Michigan elected to not guard the guy inbounding the ball (Lighty) or put any real pressure on The Villain in the backcourt. This proved to be a huge mistake, but then again "Michigan" and "huge mistake" are synonymous so that shouldn't have been much of a surprise to anybody. Once Lighty was handed the ball by the referee, he inbounded it to The Villain, and The Villain started running toward our basket to gain momentum. He took two dribbles, jump-stopped as he crossed half-court, and let a 37-footer go with Stu Douglass's hand in his face right before the buzzer sounded.

Swish.

(Well, it hit the rim as it went through the basket, but you get the idea.)

We win. Suck it, Michigan.

Our bench poured onto the court in celebration and jumped on The Villain's back, which seemed pretty poetic considering he had figuratively put the entire team on his back all season and had literally broken his back earlier in the year. Since I was in a sling and had just had surgery on my shoulder a few days earlier, I followed my teammates toward the dog pile for a few steps before realizing that that was a terrible idea. Instead, I turned to all the Michigan players somberly walking off the court and tried to do the "suck it" crotch chop in their faces, but since I was only using one arm it looked more like I was trying to throw a fistful of those little snapping firework things onto the ground than it looked like I was trying to channel my inner DX.

Since my taunting of the Michigan players wasn't really working like I had hoped, I ran toward my teammates to join the celebration, but they were still pretty rowdy, so I diverted my path and ran by the media table on the sideline and randomly started high-fiving whoever I made eye contact with. Because I wasn't celebrating with the team and was basically running around without any real purpose, a female security guard ran toward me and yelled at me to get off the court, presumably thinking I was a random fan. So yeah, that whole series of events after the buzzer sounded and I ran onto the court just might be the most awkward celebration of a game-winning shot by a player on the winning team in the history of basketball.

Either way, thanks to The Villain's heroics, we advanced to the semifinals of the Big Ten Tournament, where we matched up with an Illinois team that was desperate for a win to cement their bid to the NCAA Tournament. In that regard, the game was a lot like our game with Michigan, only the stakes for Illinois were one step higher since a win would probably put them in the NCAA Tournament and a loss would surely send them to the NIT. Because of this desperation, Illinois played us pretty well in the first half and actually led by six at halftime after our offense sputtered midway through the first half.

When the second half started, Illinois began pulling away from us, and their lead ballooned all the way up to 11 with 12 minutes left in the game. When Coach Matta reamed into us during the under-12-minute media time-out, it seemed to light a fire under our asses, because we responded by going on a ridiculous 20–0 run to take a nine-point lead with eight minutes left and all but put the Illini away. But much like Brett Favre and Kelly Kapowski's unreal body, the Illini just wouldn't quit. They came back with a 14–3 run of their own to take a two-point lead with 1:22 left. The entire second half seemed to play out like this and was essentially just a game of runs, which is a funny coincidence considering I personally had the runs while sitting on the bench but held it in because the game was close and I didn't want to miss a thrilling finish.

In the final minute and a half, we traded baskets until Illinois finally missed what would've been the game-winner at the buzzer and instead sent the game to overtime. On the one hand, this was great news because we were given second life after we nearly let the game slip away. But on the other hand, I had some pretty bad diarrhea brewing and the only reason I held it in for the final minutes of regulation was because I thought the game would be over soon. Now we were set to play another five minutes, which seemed like an eternity to hold it, but also seemed like far too little time to go to the locker room, let it all out, wipe my crack and pull up my pants with just one arm, and return to the bench to catch what promised to be a crazy ending to the game.

I decided to again hold it in and just watch the overtime because I knew that I'd be kicking myself if I missed another desperation shot at the buzzer from The Villain or anything crazy like that. This proved to be a bad idea because the game was forced into a second overtime after The Villain hit a layup with 27 seconds left and Illinois failed to get a shot off before the buzzer sounded. Since I had been holding my ass juice in for the last 30 minutes and really couldn't hold it anymore, I darted to the locker room after the over-time buzzer sounded and sat on the porcelain throne for most of the second overtime.

I tried following the game on my phone but couldn't get any reception, so I quickly did my business and returned to the bench with about 30 seconds left in the game. By that time, we had built a five-point lead and then tacked on a couple of more points shortly thereafter to secure the win. According to my teammates, nothing too crazy happened in the second overtime, which was a relief for me since it was the first time in my career that I wasn't on the bench or the court while one of my team's games was going on. Unfortunately, though, it wouldn't be the last time.

FORTY

On the back of The Villain's near-triple-double, we annihilated Minnesota by 29 in the Big Ten Tournament Championship in our next game and set the record for the biggest margin of victory in a Big Ten championship game ever, giving us a ton of confidence heading into the Big Dance. Some experts speculated that we'd be given a number-one seed in the NCAA Tournament after going 12–1 in our last 13 games and winning both Big Ten titles, but we found out later that night that we'd have to settle for a number-two seed and a trip to Milwaukee to take on UC–Santa Barbara in the first round of the tourney, where we would eventually cruise to a 17-point win, despite The Villain playing probably his worst game of the season.

The Villain bounced back in our second-round game against 10th-seeded Georgia Tech with another near-triple-double that led the way in our nine-point victory over the Yellow Jackets. The win put us in the Sweet Sixteen for the first time since 2007, when we lost to Florida in the Final Four. And after top-seeded Kansas (who was the best team in our region) was upset by Northern Iowa in their second-round game, it seemed as though our path for a return trip to the Final Four wouldn't be nearly as challenging as we had originally anticipated.

Next up was sixth-seeded Tennessee, who we were set to play in St. Louis for a trip to the Elite Eight. Coincidentally, we had played Tennessee in our last trip to the Sweet Sixteen in 2007, when we pulled off one of the most impressive comebacks in NCAA Tournament history and beat them by one in San Antonio. This particular Tennessee team was much like the one from 2007 in that while they might have been inconsistent throughout the year, they had proven time and time again that they could beat anybody in the country on any given night, so we knew we'd have our work cut out for us.

We were pretty confident we would win because we had been playing some of our best basketball of the season and, when all else failed, we had the runaway National Player of the Year on our team (The Villain would officially win the award in April) and could just give him the ball and let him take over if need be. Simply put, while Tennessee was certainly a good team, there was nothing in the week leading up to the game that even remotely had me concerned we would lose. The morning of the game, though, was a completely different story, as a serious catastrophe struck our team.

By now it should be obvious that when I say that a "serious catastrophe struck our team" what I really mean is that something bad happened to me individually but our team as a whole was largely unaffected. This time around I woke up around 4:00 a.m. on the morning of the game and rushed to my hotel bathroom because I felt sick to my stomach and needed to barf. After I puked for about a half-hour, I returned to bed and prayed that I'd feel better in the morning, but when 9:00 a.m. rolled around and I woke up to go to our shootaround, I felt ten times worse and had a throbbing headache to go along with my funky stomach.

I decided to man up and go to the shootaround because I thought if I skipped it I'd have to also skip the game, but this turned out to be a terrible decision. I became increasingly sick throughout the duration of the shootaround, to the point that I just lay on the bench for the final 15 minutes and showered myself with vomit and self-pity. Once we returned to the hotel, Vince quarantined my room and made Danny go hang out in one of the managers' rooms, gave me a bunch of meds, explained to me that I had caught the stomach flu bug that was going around the team (a handful of guys had been sick at the Big Ten Tournament, but that was two weeks earlier), and then said that unfortunately the worst was yet to come. According to him, I'd be at rock bottom about an hour before the game was to tip off, which meant I had no choice but to lie in bed all night and miss the game. I was less than pleased with this news.

As game time approached, I discovered that Vince knew exactly what the hell he was talking about because I spent most of my time leading up to the game with my head in my hotel trash can puking my brains out and questioning what life decisions I could have made differently so I wouldn't have ended up in the position I was. Further complicating things was that I was in a sling and had no use of my left arm at all, which meant, if I accidentally got puke on my shirt or something it would have to stay there because I didn't have the energy or dexterity to clean it up. It was the worst I've ever physically felt in my life, and based on the sounds I was making as I vomited, you'd have been entirely justified in thinking that either I was getting the devil exorcised out of my body through my mouth or I was Oprah devouring a heaping plate of biscuits and gravy.

Once the game finally tipped off, I didn't even really have the energy to pay all that much attention. I had the game on TV, but most of the first half was a blur for me because I was more concerned with surviving the night than I was with our team's success (selfish, I know). When the second half started, though, I had recovered enough to at least lie up in bed and yell at the TV every so often, making me feel like some sort of combination of Gerry from *Remember the Titans* and Shooter from *Hoosiers*.

It was unbearably frustrating to not be at the game, even

though I knew I would have had literally no impact whatsoever
had I been on the bench instead of in my hotel room following
Mike O'Malley's orders by "spilling my guts." (By the way, Mike
O'Malley on GUTS was Gus Johnson before Gus Johnson was Gus
Johnson, and that is a fact.) Still, I thought that if I was at the game
I could've somehow given the guys the kick in the pants that they
needed to find that last bit of strength and put Tennessee away.

After we had led for most of the second half, and really most of
the game, Tennessee took the lead from us with about six minutes
left and seemed to have all the momentum. But something clicked
and made us realize that losing the game would not be nearly as
enjoyable as winning the game, so we fought back to regain the
lead with about two minutes left. We then turned around and
handed the lead back to Tennessee, before The Villain hit a clutch
three with 44 seconds left to give us a one-point advantage.

The tension was enough to make a healthy fan feel uneasy, so it
goes without saying that I was blowing chunks while all this was
happening. Tennessee answered The Villain's three with a tip-in
off an offensive rebound and then followed that up with a huge
steal on the defensive end. After we fouled to stop the clock, they
sank two big free throws to take a three-point lead with 13 seconds
left. Our backs were against the wall, but we had been in this position before and knew that all it took was another big three to force
overtime.

We inbounded the ball to The Villain, who dribbled up the
court and picked up his dribble to fake a handoff to Jon Diebler.
Since Jon was our best three-point shooter, both Jon's defender and
The Villain's defender bit on the fake and stayed with Jon, leaving
The Villain wide open. But he had both of his feet in front of the
three-point line, so he had to pass to Kyle and get his feet situated
before he could shoot. Kyle passed it back to him in the left corner
with just five seconds left.

The Villain caught the ball, pump-faked, and then shot an
off-balance three that never had much of a chance, but he got his
own rebound after it grazed off the front of the rim. He quickly

dribbled back out to the top of the key, swung his body around to face the basket, and let another potential game-tying shot go right before the buzzer sounded. But it didn't get far because Tennessee's JP Prince got a hand on it and sent it straight up in the air.

Game over.

Season over.

Career over.

As I sat in the hotel room and watched Tennessee's bench storm onto the court in celebration, a numbness came over me unlike anything I've ever experienced before. Throughout my career, I was absolutely certain that I was going to cry if we lost in the tournament my senior year, but now that it had happened I really couldn't do anything but stare at the TV in disbelief. After all the incredible things I was able to experience over the course of my four-year career, I never could've possibly anticipated that everything would come to an end as I lay in a hotel bed in St. Louis and threw up every bite of food I had eaten from the previous week.

But that kind of sums up my entire four years at Ohio State. From start to finish, nothing about my walk-on career was typical, so it was only fitting that the ending was equally bizarre and untraditional. Plus, it was a perfect way to bring my career full circle. After all, on November 9, 2006, I spent my first official day on the Ohio State basketball team hugging a trash can as I was reminded how out of shape I was and now, exactly 1,234 days later, I was spending my last official day on the Ohio State basketball team doing the exact same thing.

Those two days of puking will forever serve as bookends for the single greatest time in my life.

EPILOGUE

Shortly after I completed my prestigious walk-on career and graduated from Ohio State, I was in the training room at the Ohio State's gym rehabbing my shoulder and missed a call from someone who claimed to represent the Harlem Globetrotters. I went back into the locker room, listened to the voice mail that he left, and immediately thought someone was playing a prank on me. I figured it was worth the risk to call back, though, so I did and soon found out that I was one of six people the Globetrotters had "drafted" and that I was invited to participate in a training camp in September.

I had the same reaction everyone else had. "The Globetrotters have a draft? And white people are allowed to play for them?" As it turned out, they had apparently had a draft since three years prior to drafting me, and there had been two other white guys who had played for them in their 84-year history. Because of the fan base I had built with my blog, and because my "Mr. Rainmaker" video successfully showed off my trick shot skills, my guess was that the Globetrotters thought I'd fit right in and could give their dying brand a shot in the arm. And for the first week after they drafted me, that's kind of what happened.

The whole "Globetrotters draft a white benchwarmer" angle became a quirky national story in the world of sports, and I gave interviews for media outlets all over the country for about a week and a half. I mean, it wasn't like I was *the story* in America or anything, but I definitely provided the Globetrotters with some good publicity for a couple weeks that they wouldn't have otherwise had. I figured that drafting me as a publicity stunt was their plan all along, but I also assumed that they would want to keep using me (and more importantly, keep using the following I had from my blog) to get as much publicity as they could for as long as they could. I quickly found out that this plan apparently made way too much sense.

A few days after our initial conversation, the Globetrotters' rep sent me a jersey with my nickname (Shark) on the back, along with a headband and two sweatbands (seriously), and then told me he'd keep in touch with me until the September training camp rolled around. This was in late June. On July 29, I hadn't heard anything from him, so I decided to send him an email to see if he had any details about the training camp or if there was anything I needed to do in the weeks leading up to the camp. He told me that "my timing was perfect" because the camp was actually being held in August and someone else with the Globetrotters had planned on calling me in the next couple of days to iron out all the details.

That call came the very next day, and much to my surprise, the "someone else with the Globetrotters" turned out to be Globetrotter legend Sweet Lou Dunbar. Also to my surprise, Sweet Lou informed me that the camp was not only going to be held in August, but it was going to be held August 5. In other words, the camp started in six days. I was so shocked I damn near spilled soda pop all over my britches. I mean, who would have ever thought that the chick from *The Ring*, who at least gave a seven-day advance notice to her victims, would be more courteous than the Harlem Globetrotters?

The short notice was compounded by the fact that I had already made plans to go to Charlotte with my brother August 4–8 to visit his friends and celebrate his birthday. My trip really wasn't *that* big of a deal, so I told the Globetrotters that I'd be able to make it up to Long Island for the camp. I asked them to book my flight to Long Island from Columbus, but to make my flight out of Long Island go to Charlotte because I wanted to at least salvage a couple days of the vacation I had planned. (Plus I had booked my flight to and from Charlotte months earlier, and it would've just been lost money if I didn't at least use the return flight to Columbus.) They said that this wouldn't be a problem.

Three days later, on August 2 (two days before I was to fly to Long Island for the camp), a different Globetrotter rep sent me a confirmation email for my flights. According to the itinerary, I was to fly from Columbus to Long Island on August 4, and on August 6 I was scheduled to fly from Long Island to—you guessed it—Raleigh, North Carolina, a three-hour drive from Charlotte. Sadly, this was just the beginning of the comedy of errors.

This flight was eventually fixed the next day, and I decided to give the guy the benefit of the doubt since he most likely made an honest mistake. I flew into Long Island two days later, and in the airport when I landed I met one of the Globetrotter coaches and another kid they had drafted. As we took a shuttle bus to our hotel, the coach asked us both a handful of questions to find out more about us and failed miserably in attempting to make sure his "who is this white dude?" thought wasn't expressed on his face when he talked to me.

We got to the hotel, and I followed the guys to the front desk and watched as they both checked in. But when it was my turn, the receptionist furrowed her brow and banged on her keyboard for at least a minute. After she had apparently exhausted all of her ideas, she looked up from her computer and said, "I'm sorry, sir, but we don't have a reservation under that name. Are you sure you didn't book the room under a different name?"

I told her that I wasn't the one who made the reservation, which meant that there was no way that the room could've been booked under my alias. But I suggested that she should still check and see if there was a reservation for "Dr. Trevor McThundercock," just in case my alias had been used for whatever reason. Just as I suspected, though, there wasn't a room booked under that name either.

I caught up with the coach and told him there wasn't a room for me, but he told me that he had nothing to do with it and I should just wait in the lobby for the guy who was responsible for arranging the hotel accommodations to show up. Fifteen minutes later, that guy finally showed up, told me there was a mix-up, and convinced me he'd take care of it. And while he did just that, I couldn't help but think that something felt a little off.

The next day, when I walked downstairs to get on the bus and head to the gym for the camp, I noticed about 15 tall black dudes congregating in the hotel lobby, and my curiosity was piqued. Upon further investigation, I learned that these guys were also taking part in the training camp and there were so many of them because, *ohbytheway*, the training camp was actually a tryout. While I wasn't exactly thrilled with this, being forced to try out after being drafted wouldn't have been a big deal if not for the fact that the Globetrotters only drafted six people, yet the number of people trying out was somehow double that. So, if there was no real distinction between the guys who were drafted and the guys who weren't, why even have a draft in the first place? Answer: because the draft gave them an opportunity to use a handful of former college basketball players to garner a little publicity.

Among the other people drafted with me were both the champion and runner-up of the college basketball slam-dunk contest, as well as a husband and wife from Montana who had been married for four years and became a national story because they both played basketball at the University of Montana at the same time. So yeah, it was kind of obvious that they were just trying to piggyback on whatever name recognition (no matter how large or small it might have been) any of us had.

I can't say I blame them. It made perfect sense to do whatever was necessary to spark some interest in their brand, and drafting all of us accomplished that. No, the issue I had was that what happened following the draft proved that either they were the most inept organization I had ever been involved with or they were just trying to exploit me. And quite honestly, I'm not sure which is worse.

The tryout was held at a local high school in Long Island, but it looked more like a run-down prison than a place for secondary education. Steel bars protected all of the windows, and a security guard protected the front entrance with assistance from a full-body metal detector. In other words, this high school was in the heart of what Will Buford would refer to as "the muh-fucking hood." It was just like the high school that all my upper-middle-class, white, suburban classmates and I went to, with the only exception being that it was the exact opposite in every way.

Since I was a marshmallow in a bag of charcoal to begin with, you can imagine how out of place I felt when I saw that the tryout was being held at Shawshank High. (I guess it's my fault for being naive and expecting anything else—after all, I wasn't trying out for the Beverly Hills Globetrotters.) We made our way to the gym of the school and were told to get warmed up while the Globetrotter reps got some things organized. Five minutes later, they told us all to go over to a table to pick up a jersey that had a number on it that made us more easily identifiable for the "scouts."

In what should come as no surprise, I was the only guy who didn't have a jersey waiting for him. I initially thought this was because I was the only white guy and therefore didn't need a jersey since I was already easy to pick out, but then I didn't see my name on the list of players the scouts had. In that moment, everything suddenly made sense. They'd had no intention of bringing me to this camp and would've let it come and go without ever telling me about it had I never emailed that Globetrotter rep to ask him what the plan was.

This explains why they gave me such short notice (they weren't going to call me until I coincidentally sent that email a week before the camp started), why they didn't have a hotel room for me, why they didn't have a jersey for me, and why my name wasn't on the roster. Shortly after putting all these pieces together, I made up my mind that no matter what happened from that moment on, I wanted nothing to do with the Globetrotters and vowed that I wouldn't play for them even if they offered me $10 million and fellatio from Curly Neal himself.

I can't get into specifics about the tryout because I signed a confidentiality agreement with the team and could face up to three buckets of confetti poured on my head if I violate it, but I can say that I hadn't yet been fully cleared from shoulder surgery and therefore couldn't take part in any contact drills at the tryout. I assumed this wouldn't be a huge deal because I've seen my share of Globetrotter performances, and there is about as much physical contact as there is at a fifth-grade dance. But surprisingly, I assumed wrong.

I couldn't participate in most of the tryout, and when all was said and done, it essentially consisted of shooting about 25 jump shots (all of which were really deep threes). Having a bum shoulder wasn't ideal, but I'd told the Globetrotters from the start that I wouldn't be 100 percent until September, so they knew what to expect.

I was a little rusty, and while I wasn't exactly terrible, my jump shot was a ghost of my usual silky smooth J. Still, like I mentioned, it's not like I provided a large enough sample size for them to make a well-informed decision (especially considering that it was only three days after I was cleared to start shooting again). But naturally, common sense wasn't about to stand in their way.

After the tryout, we were told that we'd have individual meetings with the Globetrotter coaches and front-office personnel. My meeting was set for 8:00 p.m., and since we got back to the hotel at around five, I figured I'd grab some dinner. But when I left the hotel to find a place to eat, my phone rang. "We were just wondering where you were because the coaches are downstairs waiting to have their meeting with you right now."

"Of course they are," I said. "I'll be there in a few minutes."

At this point, changing the meeting time without telling me was really just another drop of water in the ocean, but that didn't make it any less frustrating. The meeting actually went pretty well, but like I said, it was a moot point because I had already made up my mind that the Globetrotters could massage their tonsils with my balls.

I left Long Island expecting to never hear from the Globetrotters again. After all, it was pretty clear to me that they never wanted me at the tryout in the first place. Nonetheless, they told me when I left that they'd let me know about their decision in a few weeks, and strangely enough, they followed through on that promise. Some two or three weeks later, the same Globetrotter rep who had been calling me throughout the past few months was on the other end of the phone telling me that I'd be a perfect fit for the Washington Generals, which as you may know is the team that the Globetrotters play on a nightly basis and consequently dominate on a nightly basis. Doing my best to hold in my laughter, I respectfully declined. After all, this was like getting drafted by the Lakers and being asked to play for the LAPD's coed Gus Macker team instead. Anyway, in the next few months the Globetrotters called me no less than four times and asked me to either reconsider their offer or to at the very least play for the Generals when the Globetrotters came to Columbus.

Each time they called I tried my best to make it clear to them that I had no intention of playing basketball after college and the only reason I had been even slightly interested in playing for the Globetrotters was because it was such a unique and bizarre opportunity that I thought it would be fun to follow through with it. The last I heard from them was in December 2010, when I ignored an email that asked me to again reconsider their offer, and in doing so I ended my six-month affiliation with the Harlem Globetrotters.

Now that you know the whole story, let's break it down. Here's what I think happened from their perspective, although I'm probably giving them a little too much benefit of the doubt with some of this: I think they drafted me because they knew I had a cult follow-ing from my blog, they knew I was a good shooter (and specifically a good trick shot artist), and they knew I considered myself an entertainer of sorts. But more importantly, they knew that draft-ing a white guy who never played in college would generate some media interest and get people talking about the Globetrotters again.

Then, sometime after the draft, they decided that waiting for me to heal from shoulder surgery wasn't worth it and/or that they had gotten all the media attention and fan interest from drafting me that they were after. I wouldn't have had that big of a problem with this, except for the fact that they failed to relay this news to me and consequently left me hanging about what was to happen next.

My email to the Globetrotter rep put them in a bind and ruined their plan to ignore me. They most likely wanted to respond by say-ing, "Sorry, Mark, but we only drafted you for a flash-in-the-pan thing that would put us in the media spotlight for a few days. We're unfortunately going to have to tell you that we don't think you'd be a good fit for us, and we don't want to waste your time by making you come to our training camp." But instead, they shrugged their shoulders and thought, "Ah, what the hell, we might as well give the kid a shot."

They must have then scrambled to add me to everything, but somehow forgot to book me a hotel room or put my name on the roster. At the tryout, they saw me shoot a handful of threes, and since I hadn't had time to work on my shot after my surgery, I missed a little too often for their liking, and they decided that I wasn't good enough to play for them.

In my opinion, the Globetrotters' biggest mistake was thinking that I had to actually play to be effective. What they failed to real-ize was that they would have been much better off assigning me the role of "team benchwarmer" since that was what I was known for anyway. They could have made my role on their team an exten-sion of my role at Ohio State, by having me sit on the bench and either not play in the games (I could've interacted with the crowd in some fashion during the game) or only play in the final minute and make a big deal about me trying to score (or both).

Meanwhile, I could have maintained my blog and given fans the same access to the Harlem Globetrotters that I had given them for the previous two years to the Ohio State Buckeyes. In fact, even if they did think I was good enough to play for them, they still should have used this strategy. Instead, they made a series of baffling moves that still have me puzzled.

By the way, since most of you probably think I came across as a whiny asshole, it should be noted that the Globetrotters were the ones who sought me out. It's not like I'm bitter because I begged them to give me a chance and then they told me I wasn't good enough. If anything, I'm upset that they wasted my time and failed to see the potential in a partnership between us. It's not like I had planned for years to join the Globetrotters after college, so being rejected by them really had no impact on my life at all. It's like being on *The Price Is Right* and never getting off of Contestants' Row—sure it would've been nice to have a chance to win, but it was unexpected to be in that situation in the first place, so it's not like my life is for the worse now.

Anyway, just so we're clear, I'm a whiny asshole not because the Globetrotters ruined a dream of mine but because they were an unorganized cocktease and dragged me into a situation that I would've wanted no part of if I had known what awaited me. And as far as I'm concerned, that's a perfectly excusable type of whiny asshole.

Even though my time with the Globetrotters ended up being a crusty turd of an experience, it's hard to get too upset over everything. After all, if someone had told me on my first day at Ohio State that in four years I'd be drafted by the Harlem Globetrotters, I probably would have asked them why they were wasting their ability to predict the future by being my personal soothsayer and not using it to gamble or save lives like that guy from *Early Edition*. Then I would've tried to wrap my mind around how exactly a math major basketball manager and aspiring orthopedic surgeon was going to get a chance to play for one of the world's most historic basketball teams. It would've made absolutely no sense to me at that time, but that's because I couldn't have possibly known that I was about to embark on an incredible journey.

While it would've been nice to actually play for the Globetrotters, simply being drafted was enough because it validated just how amazing and unique this journey really was. I would have never thought I had even an inkling of a chance to someday get drafted by the Globetrotters or do any of the other cool things I got to do, but thanks to a combination of minimal skill, a few valuable relationships, and a whole lot of luck, I was able to achieve my childhood dreams and then some. I know exactly how blessed I am to have had the opportunities I did, and I'll forever be grateful to Coach Matta, everyone at Ohio State, and the passion of the Buckeye faithful for making it all possible. I truly will cherish every second of my four years at OSU and look back on that time with the fondest of memories, because I can say these two things with absolute certainty: there's no place on Earth like Ohio State.

And Michigan still sucks.

ABOUT THE AUTHOR

MARK TITUS is the creator of ClubTrillion.com, and a contributor at Grantland.com. He was featured several times in the *New York Times*, ESPN.com, and Bill Simmons's podcast, among others. He graduated from Ohio State in 2010, a hero to millions. *Don't Put Me In, Coach* is his first book.